The Family

Guid

Working

BY KATHY PEEL
Published by Ballantine Books

THE FAMILY MANAGER'S
GUIDE FOR WORKING MOMS

THE
Family Manager's Guide for Working Moms

KATHY PEEL

◆

BALLANTINE BOOKS · NEW YORK

Family Manager is a registered trademark of Kathy Peel

http://www.randomhouse.com

Library of Congress Cataloging-in-Publication Data
Peel, Kathy, 1951–
The family manager's guide for working moms / Kathy Peel. — 1st ed.
    p.   cm.
ISBN 0-345-41311-3 (pbk.)
1. Working mothers—Time management—United States.   2. Family—Time management—United States.   3. Work and family—United States.   I. Title
HQ759.48.P43   1997
640'.43'0852—dc21   97-20386
CIP

Cover design by Cathy Colbert
Cover photo by Matthew Barnes
Text design by Ann Gold

Manufactured in the United States of America

First Edition: September 1997

10   9   8   7   6   5   4   3   2   1

To Cynthia Romaker Fullmer

Each friend represents a world in us, a world possibly not born until they arrive, and it is only by this meeting that a new world is born. —Anaïs Nin

ACKNOWLEDGMENTS

No dual-career woman can do it alone, and I can't either. The credit for getting this book from concept to publication goes unreservedly to many people:

- Jan Johnson, book editor extraordinaire, challenges, encourages, and pushes me (sometimes hard) toward clarity and meaning. Mediocrity is not a word in her vocabulary.
- My home-office team: Holly Halverson, diva of details, without whose expert editing I would not be able to meet my never-ending deadlines; Katie Weiss, my dedicated editorial assistant, who ably juggles constant and myriad requests for help of all kinds; and Nancy Guthrie, president of Guthrie Communications, who keeps me connected with the world.
- Phil Pfeffer, president and COO of Random House and maybe the busiest person on the planet, but not too busy to advise and encourage me and to introduce me to the wonderful team at Ballantine.
- The Ballantine publishing team, with whom it is an honor and a joy to work—Judith Curr, Susan Randol, Ellen Archer, Linda Grey, Claire Ferraro, Nancy Inglis, and Alix Krijgsman.
- Marcy Posner, vice president of William Morris Agency. Her belief and encouragement go a long way.
- My greatest debt is to my husband, Bill. It's not easy being married to an entrepreneur/small-business owner/crusader/marketer/busi-

ness traveler/Family Manager. I couldn't do what I do without his love and support. I also thank my children, John, Joel, and James, who are ever-willing guinea pigs for all the Family Management principles.

THE FAMILY MANAGER'S CREED

I oversee an organization—
Where hundreds of decisions are made daily,
Where property and resources are managed,
Where health and nutritional needs are determined,
Where finances and futures are discussed and debated,
Where projects are planned and events are arranged,
Where transportation and scheduling are critical,
Where team-building is a priority,
Where careers begin and end.
I oversee an organization—
I am a Family Manager.

Contents

Starting Point

If the ants are so busy, how is it that they attend all the picnics?

"When my kids ask to take a spur-of-the-moment picnic or my husband suggests we try to make an early movie, I'm in a double bind," Jerri, a wearied sales manager, told me at a Family Manager seminar. "I feel guilty if I go because I've left mounds of laundry, unpaid bills, monthly reports, unreturned phone calls, and countless other tasks unfinished. But I feel guilty if I keep working and don't go with my family because I want to spend time with them. I can't figure out how to win." Listen carefully, and you'll hear a long collective sigh from dual-career women everywhere who know *exactly* how she feels.

Over the past ten years I've had conversations with thousands of women. Some time along the way, I began to pick up on patterns. I heard stories about similar struggles from women from Seattle to St. Louis to Tampa. They worry about their jobs, their marriages, and their children. They're distressed about the economy, the environment, and the future we're leaving to the next generation. They're concerned about local schools, their children's friends, and the values presented on TV. They feel like they don't have enough time to do everything they want to do—or even just what they think they should be doing. They tell me they've lost their sense of balance, that their days pass so quickly

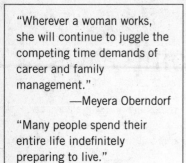

> "Wherever a woman works, she will continue to juggle the competing time demands of career and family management."
> —Meyera Oberndorf

> "Many people spend their entire life indefinitely preparing to live."
> —Dr. Paul Tournier

that they don't fully experience them anymore. Play is something reserved for children.

- When was the last time you rode a bicycle?
- When was the last time you created something with your hands?
- When was the last time you were enjoying life so deeply that you laughed out loud?
- Are *play* and *rest* words foreign to you?
- Is time your enemy?

When you get right down to it, whether we're raising teenagers in a rural community or preschoolers in a big city, whether we're doctors or dressmakers, whether we're coping with a limited income or are fairly comfortable financially, we all struggle with basically the same issues. Only the details differ.

Women on the East Coast, West Coast, and everywhere in between also share success stories. Many are already doing a good job managing a family and a career. I have to say that the bad news *and* the good news is that no one woman, of the thousands I've met, feels like she is perfect.

The problem is that perfect is the problem. Perfection is an illusion. We dream about how perfect things will be when the kids get old enough to take care of themselves, when we get a promotion, when we land a new job, when we get to quit our job, when we can buy a bigger, better, easier-to-take-care-of house. When, when, when . . . Suddenly we notice we still haven't achieved perfection and twenty years have gone by.

What about the hours and minutes between promotions and projects? How can we find fulfillment (not to mention sanity) there? How can we make life work?

Let me reassure you from the start: I am not going to tell you how you can have and do it all—maintain a sleek body, a close-knit family, a stimulating career, and a sizzling sex life—on five hundred calories a day and three hours of sleep a night. I *am* going to show you how to run your home and your life like a true manager, capably balancing the competing demands of family and career. The key word in that last sentence is *balancing*. You'll see that word a lot as you read this book because finding balance—between work and rest, structure and spontaneity,

> "It is with life as with a play; what matters is not how long it is, but how good it is."
> —Lucius Annaeus Seneca
>
> "Balance has always been necessary and will always be necessary. It is just becoming more difficult."
> —Dr. Richard Swenson
>
> "Remember always that you have not only the right to be an individual, you have an obligation."
> —Eleanor Roosevelt

giving and receiving, others and ourselves—is what makes life work. It's what makes it possible to have an efficient, smooth-running household while working at a full- or part-time career outside the home.

In the past nine years I've written twelve books and dozens of magazine articles. I've also given hundreds of speeches about women's lives now—how they are and how we want them to be. What began as a personal search has turned into something much bigger. I've written, I've talked, and I've listened. And what I've heard makes me absolutely certain of two things: our learning curve is lifelong and we are each other's own best teachers.

This book is about finding out what's most important to you and how to make decisions that reflect those priorities. It's about moving toward your dreams for your family and yourself. We'll talk along the way about how you can incorporate smart operating strategies into your life in your own way. The last thing I want to do is make everyone the same. Each of us is an individual, and each of us is a woman with two careers.

This book isn't just for women who have two full-time jobs—one at home and one in the marketplace. It's also for women who have one full-time job at home plus a part-time job in the marketplace. It's also for women who have a full-time job at home and volunteer full-time in the community. (The busiest woman I know sits on numerous community boards, spends hundreds of hours volunteering, *and* runs a home.)

This book is meant to provoke you in the best sense—that is, to provide you with ideas and concepts you can apply to your own unique life. It's not a how-to manual, but a framework for your own journey, your own path to a balanced, fulfilled life. I wrote this book out of my experience as a business owner and Family Manager, as someone who has spent countless hours helping women learn to manage their families and their lives . . . and thereby learning to manage my own.

Like you, I have a lot of desires for my life. I want to be a good wife, mother, coworker, friend, daughter, sister, and citizen. I want to be physically fit, intellectually astute, emotionally stable, spiritually grounded, socially accepted, and professionally savvy. These are lofty goals, and I've got a long way to go. I'm always looking for ways to improve.

I invite you to begin wherever you are and move forward. Keep a notebook close by to make notes to yourself about what you're learning. Use the ideas in this book as a springboard to your own ideas about how to do things even better. The more you make this book your own, the more balance you'll experience in your life.

You are obviously talented and in demand, or you wouldn't have a career and a family to manage. And you clearly care about doing both of these things well, or you wouldn't be reading this book. Please consider yourself strong, capable, and skillful. Reread that last sentence. Then let's explore how you can be as busy as an ant and still make it to the picnics!

> "You don't have a good life just because you hold good cards, but because you play well the ones you're holding."
> —Anonymous

The Family Manager's
Guide for
Working Moms

ONE
Two Jobs, One Life

"To love what you do and feel that it matters—how could anything be more fun?"
                                        —Katharine Graham

It's been a long day, but a good one. I was up at 4:50 as usual and at the YMCA to work out by 5:25. Usually there's only a handful of us crazies there at this hour, but it's early in January, so the place was packed with New Year's resolutioners. At 6:20, I headed across the street to the supermarket, then home. While I put away groceries, I listened to make sure eleven-year-old James was in the shower. I fixed breakfast and checked my calendar for the day. After finishing his morning chores, James left for school at 7:30. I cleaned up the kitchen, swept up the dog hair on the floor, made the bed, and threw in a load of laundry. I took the ground beef out of the freezer. My husband, Bill, is cooking chili tonight.

By 8:00 I was in my office, starting my other job. I've got three magazine articles due, a TV segment and a book to write, and a radio show to do. I fielded phone calls and talked to publicists, agents, and editors.

I work in a home office I share with Bill. Among my "working" women friends and acquaintances, who number in the thousands since I've started writing and talking about Family Management, I count physicians, entrepreneurs, nurses, secretaries, police officers, graphic artists, sales reps, attorneys, editors, dental hygienists, adver-

> "It has begun to occur to me that life is a stage I'm going through." —Ellen Goodman
>
> "The trouble with the rat race is that even if you win you're still a rat." —Lily Tomlin

tising executives, teachers, office managers, travel agents, ministers, physical therapists, and women whose "only" job at the moment is that of Family Manager.

The truth is, it's not two jobs, it's a life. No matter how many jobs we have, we all have only one life. It might be complex and hectic, but it's ours to make it what we will. This book is about meshing what we tend to look at as two different worlds—work and home—to create one efficient, satisfying life. It's about balancing and simplifying. I no longer separate my to-do list into work and home, or into work and a second-best other called home and family, or into home and a second-best other called work. Real life is all of the above.

That's why my to-do list on the day in question, besides the writing and the radio show, included getting nineteen-year-old Joel ready to go back to college, making dental appointments, exchanging the last of the too-small Christmas gifts, sending a get-well card to a friend, and most exciting of all—buying a new mattress pad for our bed.

Other days find me rushing for the airport, briefcase in hand, or throwing a load of laundry in the washing machine between twenty minutes on the phone with my editor and carpooling James and his buddies to the sport of the season. Often I run errands at lunchtime. Sometimes I work late into the night meeting a deadline or decorating for a party.

Sound familiar? If your to-do list is a wild mix of the essential, the mundane, and what your colleagues, clients, boss, and/or family need, you and I are in the same boat. We actually have two full-time careers, and our boat occasionally springs leaks.

Juliet B. Schor, author of *The Overworked American*, writes that women now must cope with a double share of work: the duties they assume at home and those they're assigned at work. Nearly two-thirds of all adult women are now employed, and there are almost that many moms on the job—is it any wonder we feel overwhelmed? Schor notes that our standard operating procedure is to start our days before dawn, doing whatever household chores we can accomplish—laundry, cleaning—before feeding and dressing the kids and sending them to school. We then commute to our workplaces and meet the demands thereof. After a full day there, we commute back to our "second shift"—being mom, wife, daughter, and friend. We fill the dusk-to-dark hours with grocery shopping, cooking, cleaning up. Between helping kids with school-work and bedtimes, we fit in as much housework as we can. One study calculated what this adds up to: over eighty hours a week spent on our two full-time jobs.

The Miracle of the Hats

Like you, I wear a lot of hats, and sometimes it's hard to keep them straight. A letter I received recently listed all the hats a woman is expected to wear, and wear well, in the nineties and beyond. Does this list sound familiar?

Accountant/Bookkeeper, Auto Maintenance Supervisor, Babysitter/Day-Care Worker, Building Supervisor, Filing Clerk, Chauffeur, Cheerleader, Coach/Teambuilder, Counselor, Dean of Education, Entertainment Chairman, Fashion Coordinator, Fitness Trainer, Gardener, Gift Coordinator, Health-Care Practitioner, Historian and Curator, Hotel Manager, Interior Designer, Laundress, Maid, Manager of Food Services, Purchasing Agent, Referee, Seamstress, Secretary, Travel Agent, Veterinarian

"Now, as always, the most automated appliance in a household is the mother."
—Beverly Jones

"What is important is not where you come from but where you are going."
—Bernie Rhodes

While no woman wears all of these hats in any one day, she does don each of them regularly. There was a time when I sought, with boundless determination, to fulfill all of these demands, on my own power and without a plan. From college graduation to three children and a station wagon, I was determined to be the ultimate mom—no matter what it took. And heaven knows, it took a lot. My family would confirm that many of the responsibilities that came with the hats rank right up there with astrophysics in terms of difficulty for me.

People are often shocked to hear my background. They think I'm one of those women born straightening the Q-tips on the changing table, that being efficient was in my genetic structure. Well, they're wrong. For years I was the consummate slob. Just ask my college roommates or Bill. He'll verify that early in our marriage, the floors in our house had to be raked before they could be vacuumed.

I grew up in a home where both my parents were professionals. Mother owned dress stores, complete with a full-time tailor on staff; she also had a housekeeper and cook to help at home. Consequently, I never learned to sew, clean house, or cook. I had a built-in job selling clothes at Mom's stores, so unlike my friends, I didn't babysit to earn spending money. I knew next to nothing about small children.

Complicating my domestically challenged lifestyle was the fact that I worked; part time for a while, then (and now) full time. It wasn't long before I had to admit my Get-Through-It-by-Sheer-Tenacity attitude wasn't going to work. I needed help. This is where my childhood came to serve me well.

Though I missed some domestic training from my family environment, I did pick up a lot of know-how about business—things like problem solving, team building, goal setting, research and development,

delegation, budgeting, innovation, and creativity. While other women perused tab-
loids in the grocery store checkout line, I
skimmed *Business Week*. Although initially my business background seemed use-

> "The name we give to
> something shapes our
> attitude toward it."
> —Katherine Paterson

less in the pursuit of homemaking efficiency, it became the framework
for my philosophy of home and family, the foundation for strategic
Family Management, and the salvation of my sanity.

Once I realized that the skills I picked up for running a business
could be used just as strategically to run my home, something clicked. I
saw that the term *domestic engineer* really didn't cover my duties anymore; I was, in truth, a Family Manager. The first thing I did was change
my self-perception. When I started thinking of myself as a Family Manager, it was a liberating experience. I saw the world through new eyes. I
realized that, like any manager, I needed a way to organize my head,
my day, my life. I needed to simplify. I reread my journals from past
years; in these pages I had listed goals and recorded things that worked,
thoughts that uplifted, other women's experiences that taught me something. I thought about our family routines and special demands. I initi-
ated conversations with women whose lives I admired.

Writing a Job Description

After I had been thinking about myself as a manager for a while, I took
myself, my favorite pen, and a yellow legal tablet out for a long business
lunch. I wrote down all of the chores and responsibilities that came with
my job. Drawing on my business background, I studied these activities
and tried to categorize them, putting each item on the list into a general
department. I wanted to see if any patterns emerged. They did. Seven
distinct areas appeared that made a lot of sense to me as a Family Manager. I concluded I needed a job description more detailed than the list
of hats I mentioned previously. Although I've refined and changed my

job description over the years as my sons got older, the departments have remained the same.

Time. Make sure the right people get to the right places at the right times with the right equipment. Solicit scheduling input from family members, keep a master calendar, and remind others that they are responsible for their own time.

Food. Meet the daily food and nutritional needs of my family efficiently, economically, and creatively. Delegate parts of cooking, cleanup, shopping, and meal-planning responsibilities.

Home and Property. Work with Bill in setting short- and long-term goals, such as fixing the roof and remodeling the kitchen, and in implementing the goals—e.g., getting bids, hiring contractors, getting a home-improvement loan. Maintain all our tangible assets, including our possessions, the house, and our property.

Finances. With input from other family members, set and manage monthly, annual, and long-term budgets—that is to say, create a plan to cover bills and oversee all the other monetary issues of a home. Research and implement cost-cutting and investment plans.

Special Projects. Coordinate plans for all special projects, big and small, that are outside our family's daily routine—including birthdays, holidays, vacations, garage sales, and family reunions. Plan, delegate responsibilities, implement, and evaluate at the end of each project.

Family Members and Friends. Develop thriving family life and relationships, serving as teacher, nurse, counselor, mediator, and social chairman. The responsibilities in this category include everything from taking care of Grandma as her health declines to getting to know our neighbors. Act as mentor for other team members (a.k.a. children) so they develop relational skills.

Personal Management. Arrange for my own growth and care physically, emotionally, intellectually, and spiritually. (If I don't manage myself well, I won't be able to manage anything or anyone else well!)

Many job descriptions allocate a percentage amount of the total job to the responsibilities in each category. A person like me, one who finds numbers useful on a calendar but not in a checkbook, may find this concept difficult to understand. But we all do need to think about which departments carry more weight and demand more of our time. If you're a Family Manager with three small children, as I once was, you'll probably spend more time on Food and Home and Property. As the children grow and can take over some responsibility for cooking, shopping, and doing their own laundry, you may delegate more of the responsibilities in these areas and concentrate your time on others.

In the end, a woman with dual careers trades in her twenty-seven hats, plumbing wrench, law-enforcement badge, bowl brush, wire whisk, leaf rake, leash, pager, briefcase, and sweatpants for one Family Manager hat— under which she governs all her responsibilities at home strategically.

Spend some time thinking about your role as Family Manager. If you wrote a job description for yourself today, using the seven departments as a template, what would it look like?

If you have another job besides Family Manager, you probably already have a job description. Depending on your career, profession, or industry, this description may or may not include duties in the seven Family Manager departments. But you are undoubtedly asked to manage your time, to meet schedules and deadlines, perhaps to schedule events or meetings, and maybe to generate some kind of

> "First say to yourself what you would be; and then do what you have to do." —Epictetus

YOUR JOB DESCRIPTION

Time
Food
Home and Property
Finances
Special Projects
Family Members and Friends
Personal Management

> **"A** human being should be able to change a diaper, plan an invasion, butcher a hog, conn a ship, design a building, write a sonnet, balance accounts, build a wall, set a bone, comfort the dying, take orders, give orders, cooperate, act alone, solve equations, analyze a new problem, pitch manure, program a computer, cook a tasty meal, fight efficiently, die gallantly. Specialization is for insects."
> —Robert A. Heinlein

flow chart or planning calendar. Think about what techniques from your other job you can adapt to your job as Family Manager. As you work through this book, possibly making some changes in how you do your job as Family Manager, I urge you to keep the idea of cross-pollination in mind. Always be on the alert for the tricks of one trade that can be applied to the other.

Mission Statements

As I worked to define my role as Family Manager, I began to notice business success stories. The most successful widget-making companies might expand to make widget holders, but they might get out of (or never get into) the thingamajig business. *Aha,* I thought. These companies have a mission. They know where they are going. They are flexible enough to change direction over time, as their situation changes, but they don't undertake things with no potential for furthering their original (and periodically reassessed) mission. I decided that if the best companies have a mission statement, I should, too. After studying various business mission statements, I saw that they each answered a certain list of questions. I applied them to my family:

Why does our family exist?
What are we trying to accomplish?
What do we stand for? What do we as a family believe in?

What is our basic approach to achieving our purpose?

What is the overarching purpose I have as a Family Manager?

What would I like my family to say about me when I'm gone?

What is really important to me?

Here's what I wrote:

Kathy Peel's Mission Statement

To create a home my family would describe as a great place to be; a home where family members know they are valuable, where they feel loved for who they are as individuals, where they know they belong and can grow in their separate interests; a home that is comfortable and relaxed enough for those of us who can stand clutter, and orderly enough for those of us who like everything in its place.

Okay, okay. Some of you are shaking your heads. You think I obviously don't know that Laurie Beth Jones, author of *The Path: Creating Your Mission Statement*, says a good one "should be no more than a single sentence long, should be easily understood by a twelve-year-old, and should be able to be recited by memory at gunpoint." As you can see, I had not yet put into practice the concept of decluttering—in my life or in my writing. Following Jones' advice, I wrote an abbreviated version:

Kathy Peel's Revised Mission Statement

To create a home full of love and comfort, order and flexibility, stimulation and relaxation.

As I thought about my mission for my home, I also thought about what I *don't* want it to be: a fast-food drive-through, where family members rush in, grab a bite to eat and clean clothes, ask for money, exchange a few words, and rush out again. I knew that in large part it was up to me to set the tone so this wouldn't happen.

> If you aim at nothing, chances are you'll hit it.

That's why I sought efficient, streamlined, entrepreneurial, and innovative management. I knew my mission was worth pursuing. And while we don't always live up to my ideal, we're hitting the target more often than we're missing it because we're aiming at something.

Take some time right now and begin to develop your own mission statement. Use the same questions I used to get you going.

By now you might be thinking, *Kathy Peel doesn't have enough to do. First she tells me she's going to help me make sense of my overbusy life. Then she asks me to take time I don't have to write a job description and a mission statement.* All I can say is, bear with me. Every exercise in this book, while it may take time to begin with, is something I myself have done—as have countless other women. A job description is useful because it clarifies your dual-career roles. A mission statement simply makes it easier to stay on track. It gives us an overall yardstick against which to measure the many decisions we make in a day or a week. For example, if cleanliness isn't even mentioned in your mission statement, why are you spending twenty hours a week cleaning house? If intimate communication between family members is, then why aren't you working to find ways to spend time together—maybe over dinner?

I'm not saying that having a job description or a mission statement by itself is going to make your life any more rewarding or ensure that your dual careers mesh any better. But you're going to have something to refer to, similar to a map, when the demands of your two jobs collide. Maybe it is more important for you to work long hours at your career and delegate some of the Family Management tasks to your spouse or to hire someone to help you. I think that's fine, as long as you know what your priorities are in both your jobs.

Input, Input, Input

"It's in changing the way people work that I think the answers to productivity are going to be found."
—John Sculley

Another issue people in management must take into consideration is who is on their team. Just who are they managing? There are hundreds of management books on various management styles and ways to implement them, including ways to reward and motivate people. If you are married, talk with your husband about your mission statement and your job description. Negotiate standards you'll both be able to live with, ways to work better together, and goals for "delegating" responsibilities to your children.

I assure you this will not be a single meeting. If you belong to either the "I'll Do It by Myself" club or the related "It's Only Going to Get Done Right If I Do It" sorority, you may have to adjust your own expectations. If you've always had a more traditional arrangement in which you are responsible for most, if not all, chores around the home, implementing the new system may take some persuading and negotiating. But keep after it. Consider what you're teaching your children by doing everything yourself. Think about what you want them to know about being able to take care of themselves—body, mind, and soul—later in life. In fact, I believe these considerations so important that I've devoted Chapter 5, "A Team That Works for All of You," to them.

Over time this way of categorizing my roles and responsibilities has held up for me. In my first book on this subject, *The Family Manager,* I

Do You Know Where You're Going?

Remember Alice in Wonderland, when she came to a fork in the road and asked the cat which path she should take. The cat asked her where she wanted to go and when she replied she didn't care, the cat wisely observed, "Then any road will take you there."

devote a chapter to each department. These departments have stood the test of time. I use them still. Yet even the best organization needs both fine-tuning and occasional major overhauls.

> "The only management practice that's now constant is the practice of constantly accommodating to change."
> —William G. McGowan

In the past few years, my life has changed. Two of my sons have left home for college. Both my job and Bill's have changed. Few of us who now work or have worked in the marketplace would think of taking on a new job without first looking at the job description. As we progress in our careers, taking on new responsibilities, getting promotions, or changing jobs, we expect to negotiate and sometimes renegotiate our job descriptions. We do the same at home as our situations change. If an accountant takes on the additional role of, say, corporate financial planning, she might determine who is going to take on her day-to-day accounting responsibilities, perhaps negotiating for a trainee assistant who can, over time, take over more and more of her duties as she accepts others of greater weight. Of course, our accountant couldn't justify hiring an assistant until she was clear on what her new responsibilities entailed, how much time they were likely to take, and how her new responsibilities and the possibility of hiring a new assistant fit into the company's overall goals.

As Family Managers we don't, of course, hire people to be part of our family, although, using the corporate model, we might well use freelance contractors—also known as babysitters, carpenters, housecleaners, or plumbers. We do have "trainee assistants" of one kind, though. It was quite amazing to me as my children got older how much they could learn to do and do well, sometimes better than I could. Furthermore, when the job was presented to them as one might present a job to a new hiree, in part by letting them know what's in it for them ("If we all clean the garage on Saturday morning, we can all go to the lake Saturday afternoon"), they were more than willing to undertake the task.

At the end of last summer I realized our attic had become a fire hazard. We had been piling stuff in, and every time we got a new piece of electronic anything, Bill made us save the box. I realized that if I didn't grab Joel and hire him to clean it out before he went to college, my fall decorations would never see the light of a harvest moon again. The way Joel saw it, he earned extra spending money. I got a well-organized attic. And in the end, we both got more than we expected: he uncovered a number of "missing" items I thought we'd lost, and he found "treasures" to save for his first apartment.

Simplicity Is a Balancing Act

Even with a job description, a mission statement, and built-in assistance—all essential ingredients for a dual-career woman's smooth-running home—you always need to simplify. Recently I've found myself meeting a lot more deadlines, working more at building my own business, and, perhaps as a reflection of my age and stage in life, wanting to simplify my life so that I can focus on what really matters.

I'm not saying simplicity and focus come easily to me. I frequently feel like I'm drowning in a sea of nonstop work and never-ending worries. I often find myself wishing wistfully for something fondly called the good old days when living was simpler. Uh-huh, sure it was. I quickly shake myself. If I could travel through time, would I really want to go back to some period when women built wood fires on winter mornings so the rest of the family could get out of bed? Or even to the 1950s, when women's and men's roles were more rigid and we all had fewer choices about where to live and work?

What is simpler living? Maybe simpler living in the Sunday-supplement sense means you replace all your furniture with a couple of uncomfortable high-tech

> "I believe we would be happier to have a personal revolution in our individual lives and go back to simpler living."
> —Laura Ingalls Wilder

chairs and a chic pole lamp, and pare down your wardrobe to three black dresses. That isn't what I'm looking for.

> This urge to simplify is a human impulse.

Laura Ingalls Wilder was no doubt yearning for much more than a sleek appearance; she dreamed of a better quality of life—something we all can identify with.

Ah, the good old days! No bumper-to-bumper traffic, computer viruses, long supermarket lines, voice-mail jail, broken air conditioners, and mailboxes full of solicitations for charities and catalogs offering thirty-two hundred things I don't need. Sure, deleting modern frustrations would make daily life less stressful. But I would miss the superstores where you can pick up anything from mangoes to mascara twenty-four hours a day, up-to-the-minute TV news, the Internet, electronic deposits, and my microwave oven. And when I'm pressed for time, I like having the option of getting almost anything I need delivered to my door: dry cleaning, milk, drug prescriptions, groceries, and prepared foods of every imaginable variety. There's no question that my life seems unbearably complicated at times, as I'm sure yours does as well, and there will always be times when we sit staring out the window, longing for ways to simplify. I imagine Eve did the same thing. So did Joan of Arc and Martha Washington, and so will the women of the twenty-second century. This urge to simplify is a human impulse.

Simplifying life, according to my understanding of the phrase, is not about dropping out or looking backward. It's not even necessarily about paring down or cutting back. It's about learning to choose confidently what's important and getting rid of the waste. It's about working smarter, not harder. Simplifying doesn't mean you have to quit your job, trade in your cellular phone for a washboard, or recycle your new shantung silk suit for a wardrobe of unbleached muslin. Simplifying is about attitude, a way of seeing the opportunities rather than the

> "Everything should be made as simple as possible, but not simpler."   —Albert Einstein

> "The ability to simplify means to eliminate the unnecessary so that the necessary may speak." —Hans Hoffman
>
> "Happiness is not a station to arrive at but a manner of traveling." —Margaret Lee
>
> "Objectives are not fate; they are direction. They are not commands; they are commitments. They do not determine the future; they are a means to mobilize the resources and energies of the business for the making of the future."
> —Peter F. Drucker

obstacles in our world, crammed as it is with choices and sometimes conflicts.

Sometimes, simplifying means implementing one simple idea.

In reality, few women lead simple lives. We are wives, mothers, Family Managers, and professionals. We are overworked and overwhelmed, so we attend time management workshops, study books on how to get organized, and listen to motivational tapes. What we wind up with is an I-can-do-it fever that lasts about two days tops. Then we're buried again. Maybe the reason we haven't gotten to the place we long to live in is because it's not a destination; it's a direction.

I travel a lot, and packing simply, by which I mean less—do I really need that pair of navy blue shoes?—is a goal I have. Picture this. My flight was delayed. If I ran I could catch the connecting flight. But I was trying to balance a briefcase, a large purse, a dress bag, a portable computer, and a suitcase. It suddenly occurred to me that running from terminal J to terminal Q trying to balance five bulky objects was slowing me down. *If being off-balance was complicating my life in airports,* I thought, *in what other areas of life had I become unbearably unbalanced? That,* I realized, *was the key: simplicity.* Embracing simplicity is less about trading in turn-of-the-century technology for romantic ideas of yesteryear than it is about identifying our goals and dreams and mission in both our jobs, or our one life, and balancing the various aspects so we meet our aspirations.

For women working to mesh their two jobs in a positive way, the bottom line is not perfection. Happiness is not necessarily a completed to-do list. Happiness is the outcome of good decisions made and energy spent on a common goal, all overseen by a Family Manager rich in self-knowledge, self-forgiveness, and the determination to keep trying.

> "I have learned one important thing in my life—how to begin again."   —Sam Keen

Keeping Your Balance

- One career + one home = two full-time jobs.
- Cross-pollinate: always be on the lookout for tricks of one trade that can be applied to another.
- Think out and know your mission.
- Renegotiate your job description as necessary.
- Train assistants.
- Simplify whenever possible.
- Be willing to try again.

TWO
Learning to Balance

"Insanity is doing the same thing over and over again, but expecting different results."   —Rita Mae Brown

I love pithy quotes. They're funny. They're inspirational. They make things seem easy. It may indeed be insane to do the same thing over and over again and expect our lives to be different. On the other hand, someone's got to clean the bathroom. A great deal of Family Management, or any kind of management, is doing the same thing over and over again. Try not feeding your family for a week or not turning in your monthly inventory reports to your boss. You'll get different results, all right, although probably not the ones you want.

On the other hand, there are things we can do differently to get the different results we want. You might want a child to take more responsibility for caring for his own clothes. If you've been doing your son's laundry for ten years and you continue doing that, then he's never going to learn to run the washing machine. If you're a sales manager who wants to be the director of marketing, you're probably not going to get the promotion you want by simply meeting your monthly sales quotas. On the other hand, if you get your MBA, network with your colleagues, and contribute some imaginative work, you may eventually get the promotion. Simply put, if you want things to change, you have to change the way you're doing things.

Remember the old saw: If we had some eggs, we could have some ham and eggs, if we had some ham. There are two things you need to know if you want to make some changes in how you and your family live. (And I mean anything from small changes to a major overhaul.) You have to know what you want to change and you have to know what you want instead.

> "Live out of your imagination, not your history."
> —Stephen Covey
>
> "Even if you are on the right track, you will get run over if you just sit there."
> —Will Rogers

Those who don't understand history may be condemned to repeat it, but when you're wanting to live life to its fullest, history—how things have been—is not all that pertinent. I mean, I love remembering how things were when Bill and I were first married and living on a graduate-student budget. Those were the days when we could decide on the spur of the moment to go to a midnight show, but we rarely had the money to do so. I was full of big plans and not too in touch with certain realities. There were good times and bad times. And sometimes when I'm thinking about how my life is now, I recall those times fondly. But mostly what I think is that I wouldn't want to go back to being the person I was then, living the life I did. Fax machines hadn't been invented, for heaven's sake. Like I said, when you're wanting to move forward, history isn't all that important.

What is important is figuring out how things are now and how you want them to be. That's what this chapter is about: assessing today and visualizing tomorrow. Getting on the road to a balanced, fulfilling life takes twenty-twenty vision for the way things are now and imagination for the way they could be.

One way of just sitting there is to do the same things you've always done the same way you've always done them.

The Dirty Dozen Excuses for Just Sitting There

1. It won't work for me.
2. That's just the way I am.
3. We've been doing it this way for years.
4. It won't work in our family.
5. It takes too long to see results.
6. It's beyond my capabilities.
7. I have no control.
8. I have no choice.
9. My husband will never go for it.
10. I can't change.
11. I don't have the time.
12. Maybe later.

Some true stories are stranger than fiction. I heard this one at a Family Manager seminar. A woman who worked as a manufacturer's representative for a glassware company had a very demanding job, as did her new husband, who worked as a salesman for a men's shirt company. After their honeymoon, they bought a little house. Because they were both busy, instead of washing the dishes, every time they wanted a drink, she opened up a new box of sample glasses. Instead of doing laundry, he just wore another sample shirt. After a time, dirty glasses covered every flat surface, and dirty shirts festooned all the chairs in the house. Talk about clutter! The woman who told me this story was embarrassed that things had gotten so out of hand. She had always envisioned having a tastefully decorated, carefully kept house. But she and her husband had never taken the time to set up their household, to talk about what they wanted their home to be like, not to mention to figure out who'd wash the dishes and do the laundry. She'd gotten so busy she always reverted to doing the easiest thing. The result was a household that qualified as an exhibit for Clutter R Us. Most of us can easily imagine ourselves in her shoes.

Who are you and how is your life now? As I write, I like to imagine you reading this book on the bus on the way to work, on the step machine at the gym, propped up in bed, or in your bright and cheery kitchen while you sit with a late afternoon cup of tea and dinner simmers on the stove. Maybe you're generally satisfied with your job and how you and your family are living. Maybe you picked up this book out of curiosity, with the notion of making a small improvement here or there. Maybe you're making notes as you think about what's working for you in the Family Management departments. I hope you are, and I hope you'll send them to me.

> "When the time for action has arrived, stop thinking and go in." —Napoléon Bonaparte
>
> "Discontent is the first step in the progress of a (woman) or a nation." —Oscar Wilde

Or maybe your life feels like a big tangled-up ball of yarn, and you can't find an end to even begin untangling it. Lots of women I know use that ball-of-yarn metaphor. One woman I know says her ball of yarn has several different ends hanging out. Her children are in high school; she's back in college getting a graduate degree and thinking of changing careers; her husband is dissatisfied with his job; and they're thinking that eventually they'd like to move to the country and start a new business. But right now doesn't feel very good to her. She can't seem to get started because she doesn't know which piece of yarn to begin with.

Maybe your house qualifies for the mayor's Clean Up the City campaign. Maybe you've thought of volunteering to be the poster child for the Domestically Challenged. Maybe *organization* is a word you're trying to learn how to spell. Maybe the last time you saw your ironing board was the day you watched Jimmy Carter's inauguration. (Actually, that's not necessarily a bad thing. Ironing isn't all it's cracked up to be.)

On the other hand, maybe your career is on the fast track, and you'll be ready for the photographer from *Perfection* magazine as soon as you finish the interview for the "Amazing Women Who Have It All Under Control" feature. You've risen professionally, you tell them, by dividing every day, including Saturday and Sunday, into fifteen-minute segments. You've just finished a big project, and after the reporter and the photographer leave, you're going to redecorate the front hallway and clean out your basement.

The photographer arrives. Your house looks beautiful, immaculate, pristine. The sun reflects off the Chippendale dining room table. The daffodils in the window box in the kitchen are in full bloom. The photographer is quite taken with your cunning revolving spice rack, with everything from allspice to tarragon stored in alphabetically arranged containers you labeled yourself. You think it would be going too far to show him your lingerie drawer with neatly folded panties color-coded according to the day you wear them. But you will show him your closet, also color-coded, with the little labels on the hangers where you record the occasions when you wore that outfit. (It wouldn't do to wear the same thing with the same people too frequently, would it?)

But who are those strangers sitting in the family room? Wait, they look familiar. Oh, yes, they're your husband and children. My goodness, the little one seems taller than the last time you saw her. Now she's whipping out her Day Runner and asking you to make a lunch date with her. You settle on a month from Tuesday.

Yes, it's possible to exaggerate. But it's also possible to be too buttoned-down, so organized and scheduled that you've forgotten that you ever heard the word *spontaneous*.

Learning Balance: Assess the Now and Envision the Then

STEP 1. DISCOVERING THE NEED FOR BALANCE (THE HARD WAY)

Maybe since I have some extra years under my belt as I raise my third child, I understand more fully that life is about assessing, adjusting, risking, and learning to balance. That's one of the reasons why when James, my youngest, took up in-line skating this year, I decided to as well. I've always been a risk taker at heart. I spent a lot of the summer vacations of my childhood roller-skating at speeds the manufacturers had not intended. *So what if thirty some odd years have passed? Learning to use in-line skates will be no problem for me,* I confidently told myself.

> "Evaluation is a time for accounting; for comparing actions with consequences; for detecting flaws and making improvements; for planting the seeds of future challenge."
> —Don Koberg and Jim Bagnell
>
> "Great successes never come without risks."
> —Flavius Josephus

Wrong. You probably already know this, but in-line skates are different from the old four-wheel roller skates. The new skates, or blades, are sleeker and faster. Instead of brakes on both toes, they have only one brake, on the heel of the right skate. It's difficult, to say the least, to stay balanced on them, especially when you're trying to slow down.

On our first day out, James latched his skates, took off, and was whizzing around like a pro in no time. I, on the other hand, learned the hard way that I should have practiced braking first. Every time I tried to stop I lost my balance. Trust me, it hurts a lot more for a forty-six-year-old woman to fall down in the middle of a street than it did for a ten-year-old girl to fall down on the smooth hardwood floor of a roller-skating rink. All of a sudden, instead of enjoying this new challenge and James's company, I could think of nothing except how much it would cost in money, time, and lost mobility to set a broken bone.

So what should I do? Give up because it's too risky or too hard?

> "Try new things and always be ready to lay yourself on the line."   —Judy T. Hoffman
>
> "Oh, the wild joys of living!"
>   —Robert Browning

(Maybe I would have if it had been something I really didn't want to do. But I really wanted to do this.) Or approach the braking problem slowly, learning to watch my speed and stop at natural plateaus and improving a little bit at a time?

I'm thinking that life is a lot like my skating dilemma. Now that we've grown up, it seems we've been thrown out of the rink onto the street. And it's a busy street. The pace is faster and the equipment is sleeker. We're taking the curves at breakneck speed, many times feeling out of control and not knowing how to stop. We can't seem to keep our balance. We fall, crash, skin our knees and emotions regularly. But isn't the solution the same?

Maybe it's time we practiced learning to brake in life, too: look for some natural plateaus to slow us down; learn some simple techniques so we can enjoy gliding along in the company of those we love; feel the wind against our faces and use gravity and momentum to our advantage. Sure, we hit some bumps and take some falls, but we're prepared to get up and go on. Yes, Rollerblading and life, especially for a woman with two careers, take a lot of energy, endurance, and balance, but they both can become an exhilarating ride.

STEP 2. FIGURING OUT WHAT BALANCE IS

Finding our balance won't keep us from falling every time. But living in balance can help us cut down on broken bones and bruised psyches. Balance is about understanding that you allocate time for personal growth—exercise, learning new things, time with friends—and that's equally as important as setting up a staff meeting at the office or shopping for groceries. Balance is understanding that it's just as important to be spontaneous and flexible about family outings as it is to have a structured morning routine that reduces stress. Balance is finding some middle ground in your family's definition of *clean* so the neatniks and the Sloppy Joes and Janes can live in harmony.

Balance means not just *spending* time, but *investing* it toward a desired end. Balance brings chaos under control.

> "There is always hope for an individual who stops to do some serious thinking about life."   —Katherine Logan

You've probably figured this out by now, but you can't stop everything to assess where you are and visualize where you want to be. Life will go on while you're assessing how your life is going, and whether you do it or not.

STEP 3. ASSESSING THE NOW

Now, right now, take the time to assess how each department in your personal Family Management domain is running. You don't have to have a master's degree in psychology or human resources. Simply jot down one or two sentences, maybe the first that come to mind, that characterize how you see things happening around you. Be ruthlessly honest about the bad and the ugly, but also about the good.

I know one woman who decided to get her life organized around the seven categories. She went out and bought herself a fancy three-ring binder. She used dividers to create separate categories and inserted paper into each. Then she made herself a table of contents so she could find each category easily. Then she began writing down every single thing she could think of that took up too much time in her life, that she didn't spend enough time on, or that she wanted to change. That's about as far as she got because the process made her so depressed. She told me just the other day that she feels guilty every time she looks at the notebook gathering dust on the bookshelf in her den.

I don't expect your one- or two-line assessments to reveal total disaster. But if you find yourself concentrating on what's wrong, you might in fact want to do this exercise twice, the first time to figure out what's wrong, the second time to recognize what's right. Here's an example to get you started.

Seven-Department Now Assessment
(A Comparative View)

NEGATIVE	POSITIVE

NEGATIVE

Time. I hate mornings at our house. We rush around, everyone's grumpy, and we leave the house on a negative note.

Food. Everybody in the family complains regularly that they don't like what's for dinner. But in the morning when I ask them what they want, nobody can ever think of anything.

Home and Property. We have too much stuff. The only way it will ever get dusted is if I open the windows and pray for a gale.

Finances. I never know when we'll run out of money and have to dip into savings. I live in fear we'll have an emergency and won't have enough to cover it.

Special Projects. Holidays and birthday parties just about send me over the edge. On top of everything else I have to do, I just can't pull off the occasions the way my mother did when I was young.

Family and Friends. I live under a load of guilt because my mother-in-law

POSITIVE

Time. I always pick up my child's car pool. I've been late a few times, but I've never missed an appointment with a teacher. I'm really good about making pediatrician and dentist appointments.

Food. My husband cooks pancakes every Saturday morning. It's become a family ritual that I, my kids, and their overnight guests look forward to. The kids now make their own lunches.

Home and Property. The roof isn't leaking. My car is running; I make sure to take it in for regular oil changes. The kids have gotten better about cleaning up their rooms.

Finances. I've set up a file folder for bills. When they come in the mail, I put them in the file. I go through the file once a week, and the rest of the time I don't worry that I'm forgetting something.

Special Projects. I organized a family reunion for seventy-five people using a planning sheet I got from a friend whose work is creating publicity events. It went off with almost no hitches.

thinks I ignore her, my husband is tired of me hitting my total-and-complete-exhaustion level every night at nine, and my kids say everyone else's mother volunteers to do stuff but me.

Personal. I always thought I'd do something great, like discover a cure for cancer, but I never could decide what to do. Now I feel like my life is getting away from me.

Family and Friends. A woman on my block organized once-a-month potluck dinners. They've become a "don't miss" on our family calendar. I plan a date for my husband and me once a month.

Personal. I go to a gym in my office building four days a week. It takes a while to finish books, but I do read them for pleasure.

My own quest to lead a balanced life has always included spirituality. And in the Bible, much to my delight, I found a most inspiring description of a Family Manager. This woman appears in the book of Proverbs. She was a diligent, multitalented worker, not only at home but also in her career and the community. In a day when women were considered nothing more than property, she had several entrepreneurial ventures going in real estate and textiles while managing her family estate well. She obviously made good use of her time. In order to accomplish so much, she must have been extremely focused on what she envisioned for her life. As busy as she was, though, she did not neglect her husband or her children.

> *A wife of noble character who can find?*
> *She is worth far more than rubies.*
> *Her husband has full confidence in her*
> *and lacks nothing of value.*
> *She brings him good, not harm,*
> *all the days of her life.*
> *She selects wool and flax*
> *and works with eager hands.*

She is like the merchant ships,
  bringing her food from afar.
She gets up while it is still dark;
  she provides food for her family
  and portions for her servant girls.
She considers a field and buys it;
  out of her earnings she plants a vineyard.
She sets about her work vigorously;
  her arms are strong for her tasks.
She sees that her trading is profitable,
  and her lamp does not go out at night.
In her hand she holds the distaff
  and grasps the spindle with her fingers.
She opens her arms to the poor
  and extends her hands to the needy.
When it snows, she has no fear for her household;
  for all of them are clothed in scarlet.
She makes coverings for her bed;
  she is clothed in fine linen and purple.
Her husband is respected at the city gate,
  where he takes his seat among the elders of the land.
She makes linen garments and sells them,
  and supplies the merchants with sashes.
She is clothed with strength and dignity;
  she can laugh at the days to come.
She speaks with wisdom,
  and faithful instruction is on her tongue.
She watches over the affairs of her household
  and does not eat the bread of idleness.
Her children arise and call her blessed;
  her husband also, and he praises her.

"Many women do noble things,
   but you surpass them all."
Charm is deceptive, and beauty is fleeting;
   but a woman who fears the LORD *is to be praised.*
Give her the reward she has earned,
   and let her works bring her praise at the city gate.
     (Proverbs 31:10–31, New International Version)

Bill wrote and framed his own version of this story from Proverbs for me for our twenty-second anniversary. It's something I look at when I'm feeling out of balance and frustrated about not being able to get everything done. I keep this hanging on the wall in my dining room. Here's an excerpt of Bill's version.

Kathy . . .
She is like a department store
   gathering all that her family needs.
She gets up while it is still dark.
She shops before dawn and provides food for her family.
She considers an idea and sells it to a publisher;
   she returns her profits to develop more business.
She sets about her work vigorously,
   spending long hours writing and speaking.
She sees that her work is profitable, and her lamp burns long
   into the night.
In her hand she holds the "mouse"
   and presses the keys with her fingers. . . .
She watches over the affairs of her household
   and does not waste time watching soap operas.
Her boys arise and tell her, "Mom, you're cool!"
Her husband also tells her she's wonderful. . . .

"Nothing happens unless first a dream."   —Carl Sandburg

"Saddle your dreams before you ride 'em."   —Mary Webb

Every time I read this, I find myself counting my blessings and my accomplishments rather than my frustrations and shortcomings. Rather than be intimidated by the woman in Proverbs, we should begin to see ourselves as much like her. We have similar responsibilities, and we no doubt handle some of those very well. In those areas where we are weaker, she can be a role model and an inspiration.

STEP 4: VISUALIZING THE THEN

I'd like to be able to tell you that I have discovered a foolproof, fail-safe way to visualize and create what I want for myself and my family. But, alack and alas, the other day when I was chasing the dog through the house, he bumped into the shelf where my crystal ball was sitting, and it fell to the floor and shattered. I was sweeping up glass for hours.

Seriously, we all know there's no one sure way to visualize what we want our lives to be, to articulate our dreams. But if we don't figure out how we want things to change, change will just happen to us. Of course, there are alterations in our situations over which we have no control. We all have givens; we all encounter unforeseen setbacks and opportunities. But if we have visualized what we want our lives to be like, we can respond more effectively to setbacks and are in a position to take advantage of opportunities.

Short of being able to create best-selling fiction and then live our lives in a novel of our own creation, the best way I know of to visualize the future is a two-step dance called Finding Congruency. Here's how it goes. First, you take each of the seven categories and list what you'd like your life to be like in them. Don't think about obstacles or make excuses about why something can't change. Simply give your imagination free rein. Here's an example.

Seven-Department Dream List

Time and Scheduling. To have family dinners together five nights a week, with time for talking about our days.

Food. To never again run out of milk at seven o'clock on a busy morning. To learn to cook low-fat gourmet food.

Home and Property. To refinance our house so we can redecorate the living room and redo the kitchen and bathrooms.

Finances. To save money for the college fund.

Special Projects. To take a family vacation that has something in it every one of us loves to do.

Family and Friends. To make more time to see old friends.

Personal. To get a graduate degree and change careers.

I invite you to take some time right now. Give yourself at least half an hour to begin. But know that you'll be able to come back to this task; in fact, you'll probably want to do so periodically. Think about your own evaluation and what you envision for your family. Be prepared for false starts because you may not be accustomed to the thought of envisioning what you'd like your family and your life to be like. This process may stretch out over days or even weeks. But keep your notepad handy. Whenever something pops into your head that describes your ideal family, whenever you see someone living out the role of a dual-career woman well, whenever you aspire to be like someone who seems to be busy and still enjoying life to the fullest, note that down, especially if you're having difficulty thinking of specific dreams for the different aspects of your life.

Here are some questions to ask yourself. They're not all department-specific, but they may help lead you to articulating specific dreams.

- What would my life and my family look like if everything were in focus and in balance?

- What do I want my children to remember about our home and family when they grow up?
- How do I want my family and friends to describe me when I die?
- Are my dreams for my family's best, or for my own ego?
- How can I use my skills and talents to enhance the quality of our life?
- Does my family agree with my goals?
- If my family was operating at peak performance, what would they look like? Our home? Meals? Recreation?
- Do I have a loving relationship with my spouse? How could I make my marriage better?
- Am I the parent I really want to be? Do I have a good relationship with each of my children?
- Do I have friendships that support and encourage me?
- Are we comfortable financially? What would make me feel more secure?
- Am I satisfied with my schedule and my family's? How could these be better?
- What supposedly impractical things have I always wanted to do for my home, my family, or myself, but felt I couldn't? Are there legitimate reasons holding me back?

Like the assessment of things as they are now, a dream list is not cast in stone. You can and probably will want to revisit your list as you and your family change. Once you've got your Dream List in place it's time to go back to your Now Assessment, both the positive and the negative. Begin to look for relationships between the two lists. What you're looking for is matches and divergences. You're likely to find some close matches and some wide diver-

> "Always bear in mind that your own resolution to success is more important than any other one thing."
> —Abraham Lincoln

gences. Those are the places to start moving forward a day and a task at a time to mesh your now and your future.

Here are some examples of how to proceed.

Look for the wide divergences. Suppose your mornings are chaos and you dream of having family sit-down breakfasts. Once you know what you have and what you want, you can take steps to get it. In this case, you might do simple things like laying out children's clothes the night before and setting up a shelf in the entryway for school backpacks, sports equipment, and anything your children need to take with them in the morning. Over time, make it each child's responsibility to put her or his possessions in the take-away place. Ask your children in the early evening if there are special things they need for school the next day— perhaps a signed permission slip for a field trip or toothpicks for a science project. Set the table for breakfast after the dinner dishes are done.

If you said under Home and Property that you want your closets to be cleaned out, but if on your Dream List, a neater, cleaner house doesn't come up at all, perhaps you still hear your mother talking in your head about clean closets. There's no congruency here. Maybe you don't really care about how your closets look and you should just concentrate on your Dream List. The closets can wait; just keep the doors shut.

If what you want for yourself is more time to spend exercising or in quiet reflection, but you find you can't do either because it's crazy when you get home from work at night, you might consider getting up earlier in the morning, before the family arises, to have your quiet time, or taking time during the middle of the day to exercise, or alternating late-afternoon child care and dinner preparation with your husband so you each get some personal time at the end of the day. I know one woman who needed some time to recharge and shift gears at the end of a hectic day in the office. Her husband often worked late, so trading off with him wasn't an option. One day she hit on a solution that, while not perfect, certainly made their evenings run more smoothly. Every day when she and her daughter got home, instead of her going immediately to the kitchen and starting dinner, they sat down in the den. Her little girl either watched *Sesame Street* or drew in her special notebook, which was reserved for this quiet time. They agreed they'd tell each other about their days at the end of the quiet time as the mother worked preparing dinner. Oddly enough, her daughter, who was then five and in school in the mornings and in day care in the afternoons, seemed to relish the quiet time as well. This solution might not work for a family with several children or if you are the sort of woman who likes to concentrate on cooking while you're fixing dinner. The point in this exercise is to look at your assessment and your visualization and try creative solutions where you find discrepancies between the two.

Look at your close matches to find these solutions. If, for example, in your Personal category, you say in the now that you like your job but wish you had more responsibility, look closely at what it is you like about your job and use that to figure out how you might get a promotion or a better job that allows you to do more of the things you like.

Or if you love spending time with friends but don't have the time, money, or inclination for more formal entertaining, look at the times when you and your friends enjoyed each other's company. What made those times special? Was it that everybody brought food? Was it that they were planned ahead? Or done on impulse? Whatever you discover, do more of what works for you.

Be Prepared:
Change Follows Change

If there's one thing I've learned about dreaming about making changes and then beginning to make them, it's that change follows change. Once you've written down your dreams, watch out, because in all likelihood what will happen is that you'll find yourself consciously or unconsciously moving toward them. Your life will change.

"Be careful what you ask for. You might get it."—Chinese proverb

This proverb sounds so simple. At one level, it's cautionary, of course. You might not like what you thought you wanted. That interpretation is, I think, especially germane in our society, where we tend to pay more attention to goals, end product, results, than to the journey along the way. And then we wonder why we don't feel happy when we get there—to the better job, the bigger house, whatever.

Another way to read the proverb is to see it as saying that if you take care with

> "The moment you alter your perception of yourself and your future, both you and your future begin to change."
> —Marilee Zdenek

> "I learned this, at least by my experiment: that if one advances confidently in the direction of his dreams, and endeavors to love the life which he has imagined, he will meet with a success unexpected in common hours."—Henry David Thoreau

> "Be not afraid of growing slowly; be afraid only of standing still."
> —Chinese proverb

what you ask for, you are likely to get it. To me, taking care means considering carefully what's in my family's best interests and mine. Again, pay more attention to the road, to living a balanced life, than to material ends.

Whether it's finding new ways to do things or employing the same techniques in new areas, you *can* expect different results. One day at a time, one problem at a time, getting better all the time, going forward despite setbacks toward the dream you visualize for yourself and your family: that's what balance is all about.

Keeping Your Balance

- Practice braking slowly. What are some natural plateaus you can use to help break your speed?
- Remember, history isn't as important as the future. Move toward it.
- Create a plan before dirty glasses and unwashed shirts create a cave you can't get out of.
- Beware the allure of the fast track. Measure its costs carefully.
- Don't let others' voices cloud your Dream List. Make sure the list is true to *your* dreams and standards.
- Welcome changes. See them as the wheels to your dreams.

THREE
Decide What's
Important

"Things that matter most must never be at the mercy of things that
matter least." —Goethe

My youngest son is living in a different situation than his older
brothers were living in when they were his age. Somewhere
between John, now twenty-three, Joel, now nineteen, and
James, now eleven, I lost my ambition to be named Room Mother of
the Year. When John was younger (as was I), I volunteered to coordinate
every class fund-raising project, drove on every field trip, and showed up
at every school party armed with cupcakes, punch, and fabulous games
and prizes.

No more.

It's not that I'm burned out. I sincerely enjoy participating in my children's activities. Their schooling is important to me. I am always available to help with homework. I provide James with all the books and
other tools he needs. I see the boys' education as their career, even though
they don't get a paycheck. And it's just as important as my or my husband's work.

And I don't think it's my age, because I feel healthier, in better shape,
and more energetic than I did ten or even twenty years ago.

No, I think I'm making different choices because with age usually

When to Be Present

As a dual-career mother, I can't attend every school function. Here's my list of no-miss events. Let these ideas help you decide what's important to you and your child.

- The drop-off and pick-up on the first day of school
- Homecoming talent show
- The Christmas play
- One field trip during the year
- Any concert, assembly, or performance in which my child has a significant role
- Parents' open house
- As many athletic games as possible in which my child participates
- Graduation or another important end-of-the-year celebration

If you can't be at an important event, call a relative or close friend to stand in for you. If possible, have him or her videotape the event so your whole family can enjoy it together later.

comes at least a little wisdom. I now have two full-time jobs and a more realistic sense of who I am and what I can accomplish. I know I simply can't do it all. But I can do a lot, and my definition of a lot has changed. One of the benefits of getting older is knowing more about who I am and what I am good at—that is, the things I can do that make a positive difference in the world, in the lives of my family, and in my life. I think I have a better grip on what's important to the people I live with. I've established priorities and I'm at peace with them. I may therefore choose not to be James's omnipresent room mother, but I will strap on a helmet and ride a bike to be with him. I may spend less actual time with him, especially in group situations, but the quality of time we spend with each other has increased dramatically.

When we don't think about what's

> "We move through life in such a distracted way that we do not even take the time and rest to wonder if any of the things we think, say, or do are *worth* thinking, saying, or doing." —Henri J. M. Nouwen

worth thinking, saying, or doing, we find it easy to get sidetracked. Sociologists tell us that something is a god, an object of worship, when it becomes the source of our self-worth and the ultimate consideration in our decision making. Our job becomes our god when we are willing to sacrifice health, family, and even ethical standards to get to the top. A woman's social status becomes her god when she chooses to snub old friends who can't help her get into a certain club or organization in favor of those who can. We can put only one thing in the top slot of our priority system. Whatever is in that place dominates everything else in our life.

> "Year by year we are becoming better equipped to accomplish the things we are striving for. But what are we actually striving for?"
> —Bertrand De Jouvenal

Every culture has stories that operate both to define the culture and to perpetuate it. The stories that define our culture are built around lofty and inspirational themes, among them freedom, a can-do attitude, and family values.

Yet somehow in our society position, possessions, and power have become the must-haves in order for us to call ourselves successful. And many men and women will do anything to get them. Let me explain what I mean by these.

Position. People must look up to and envy the station you have achieved, so you must work to achieve a station that people will look up to. It's not enough to be simply a professor or a CEO. One has to become head of the department at one of the ten best universities or chief executive at the fastest-growing company in the state. Even children see the importance of position. They want to be the most popular or the class president. Ask them why these positions are so important, and their answers boil down to some version of "It will look good on my résumé." That is, "I'll get into a better high school or college or people will think well of me." We're raising children to get their sense of self-worth from who the world says they are.

> "Don't just grab the first thing that comes by. . . . Know what to turn down." —Will Rogers
>
> "To be nobody but yourself in a world that is trying its best night and day to make you everybody else is to fight the hardest battle any human being will fight and keep on fighting." —e. e. cummings

Possessions. We must own the right house in the right neighborhood, drive the right car, and wear the right clothes—more expensive clothes than everyone else's, of course. If you wonder if you've succumbed to this value, ask yourself why you bought the last car you did. Because it has features that would make your daily life easier? Because it's rated high on performance and gas mileage? Or because it's a status symbol? We all make fun of buying things for status reasons, and yet we all do it. I would be the last to say that buying a good brand of something, even if it is more expensive, is intrinsically a bad thing. I'm simply concerned that we seem to be becoming increasingly motivated not by quality and need but by status.

Power. In general, we calculate our power in society by how many people say, "How high?" when we say, "Jump!" We're very fond of numbers. Power over others can be calculated in terms of money and bottom-line results. A person who can wipe out a small business in one fell swoop by buying it and incorporating it into his or her conglomerate—now there's a powerful person. Power over others is seductive. It gets us first-class airline tickets and the best seats in restaurants. When we have power over others, they beg to do our bidding . . . until our backs are turned one day. Then they steal our power. And the vicious cycle goes on. That's because this kind of power, "power over" someone else, is based on a zero-sum model. There's only so much of it, so to get some for yourself, you have to take away somebody else's. This kind of power goes to the biggest kid in the sandbox or the one with the most toys.

But there's another sort of power—one, in fact, that lots of cutting-edge businesses are talking about these days. When people share power, decisions are made jointly, and the people who make these decisions buy into them in a way that earns them the power to carry them out. Someone with power over others acts differently in any given situation from someone who shares power. The person who has power over others hoards the power in an effort to keep it close and unthreatened. The one who shares power sees power increase as it's used, because more people benefit from it.

> "Power is not an end in itself, but is an instrument that must be used toward an end."
> —Jeane Kirkpatrick
>
> "It is part of the cure to wish to be cured."   —Seneca
>
> "If you let decisions be made for you, you'll be trampled."
> —Betsy White

Determining our priorities—what's most important to us from the most theoretical parts of our lives (why we do the things we do) down to the nitty-gritty practical parts (what we do and how we do it)—really boils down to our choices. We must decide what's most important to us, identify *our* values, not our best friend's or boss's values or the results of somebody's latest poll of what other women value.

We live in an age of data overload. Every day we're bombarded with information intended to help us form our priorities and move us to make decisions. Television and glossy magazine ads make real life seem dim in comparison to make-believe spotless kitchens, professionally organized closets, and women still perfectly dressed and coiffed after a long day's work. Our newspapers bombard us with stories concerning how we should live now. We can find books on topics our ancestors never even heard of. And if we're not hooked up to the Internet, we're *way* behind the times. I'm not saying information per se is a bad thing—far from it. But it must be filtered. There are some things I simply don't need to know.

Six Benefits of Establishing Priorities

Simply trying to establish priorities and live by them made a huge qualitative difference in my own life. Establishing priorities helps you to:

1. *Clarify what matters most, what you want for your own life and your family's lives.* This will help you decide what you're willing to give up or add on in order to have what's important to you. Sometimes this isn't easy. Recently some good friends of ours held a fabulous weekend celebration of their twenty-fifth anniversary. They wanted out-of-town friends to come to their party, so they offered to pay for everyone's airfare and hotel accommodations. This was a wonderful invitation that we would have loved to accept, but we had a problem. One of our priorities is to spend fun, quality time with our kids. We had scheduled a weekend trip with James. We had made a commitment to James, and because of our work schedules, there simply wasn't another time to do it. We were sorry to disappoint our friends, but that was one of those tough life choices we had to make and one we felt certain about.

2. *Focus your time, energy, and resources.* When you know how you want to use your resources—for example, this year you've decided to give your charitable donations to Habitat for Humanity and your church—you won't feel guilty when the twenty-third telemarketer calls (at dinnertime) to ask you for money for the college alumni fund. Or if you've decided to make it a priority to spend quality time alone with each of your children every week, and you're offered a promotion at work that will give you a raise but will also require more hours at the office, it won't take you long to make up your mind.

3. *Know when to drop activities, and which ones, when you feel overloaded with responsibilities.* I recently talked with a writer friend who spent many hours a week working to improve conditions at her daughter's urban high school. She wrote brochures and grants, spent hours in planning meetings, and donated time to teach students writing. She did

Things I'd Have Time to Do
If I Lived by Priorities

- Putter in my yard, plant a small garden
- Spend a romantic evening with my husband
- Take more bubble baths
- Be in a better mood when I pick up my kids at school
- Enroll in the dance class I've always wanted to take
- Swim three times a week at the YMCA
- Finish the needlepoint pillow I started five years ago
- Curl up with a cup of tea and read a book for pure enjoyment
- Start a new hobby or project with my child
- Spend time reminiscing and organizing family photo albums
- Take my child on a spur-of-the-moment bike ride
- Call an old friend and catch up
- Enroll in a class and work slowly, but surely, toward my master's degree

all this for two reasons: she values public education and she wanted her daughter to have the best high school experience possible. A few years after her daughter graduated, my friend stopped working for the school. She told me she still values public education, but she's decided that for the time being, she needs to apply her limited time and energy to other causes.

4. *See how added responsibilities will affect the quality of your life in other areas.* Another friend who is a doctor has been pressured to join an HMO or a PPO—after all, that's where health care is going, everyone is doing it, and she could see more patients and make more money. So it must be right. Right? She doesn't think so. Years ago, she decided that in her practice of medicine she would care for people as a whole—body, mind, and spirit. That priority led her to take on a limited number of patients with each of whom she can spend more time. Also, she decided to limit her practice and keep control of her workload so that she could spend more time with her family. These priorities help her stick with her decision to remain independent and keep her focused on what she wants to do.

5. *See the forest when you're lost in the trees.* Especially when we have young children, this can be hard to do. We know that we want and need to spend time with our children, and that they won't be young forever. But we also know that if we completely neglect our own interests, our careers, or our personal development, we won't have much to offer our kids. I know of one young Family Manager who chose to work at home after her daughter was born. She and her husband discussed this decision at length. She's a graphic designer and he's a college administrator, so he couldn't really work at home. After two years of this arrangement, though, she was feeling totally stifled. She did a lot of soul searching and sought advice from others who were or had been in a similar situation in order to find a creative solution that would meet her priority of spending the best time she could with her daughter yet finding time to nourish herself. First, she and her husband found a part-time day-care center. Their daughter thrived, learning how to interact with other children and avoiding the only-child-as-center-of-the-universe syndrome her parents had been worried about. With the time gained from day care, this woman took on more interesting and lucrative freelance work, which made her feel, she said, like a member of the human race again. Then she got invited to enroll in a master design class that met all day on Saturday once a month. Again, after much discussion with her husband, she decided to take the class. He committed to being the primary parent for those days, giving him a whole new relationship with his young daughter, something that has pleased him greatly.

No, everything is not perfect. My friend still talks about how she'd like to have more time to pursue her own art. And her husband talks about how he's had to give up seeing his wife one Saturday a month. But they're both comfortable that they made the best long-term investment of their time in their family and themselves.

6. *Maintain your motivation.* When our priorities are in place we can see where we're going, even through tears of frustration and disappoint-ment. We've all heard stories about middle-aged people burning out. In fact, some of us have lived through them. We've all heard about the man who gets the job, title, money, and possessions he's been working for for twenty years, telling himself it was all for a family who barely recog-nize him. Then he has a heart attack or buys a red convertible and leaves his wife and kids for a younger woman. Or the woman who's so busy making a clean, picture-perfect house that her teenagers wash the pan the brownies get made in before they eat the warm brownies. These kids want to be almost anywhere but home, and their mother scarcely knows them. Or the woman who's bored and lonely and spends hours on the Internet meeting someone who "really" understands her, then leaves her family to pursue this newfound love interest.

Too often we think of *priority* as a synonym for *goal*. It is not. A pri-ority is one of a set of values, something we consider worth sacrificing for. A goal is something we strive to achieve based on our priorities. Even so, things can easily get out of sync. Say, for example, our priority is to provide our children with the best possible start in life and our goal based on that is to earn the most money to buy them the best of every-thing. Our priority and our goal don't mesh. And our children, given the chance to discover who we really are, might rather have more of us and less stuff. If the goal matched the priority more closely (we're all suscep-tible to position/possessions/power pressure), the man with the red con-vertible and the woman with the Internet-trophy husband might have enjoyed long, happy relationships and family lives with the people they married in the first place.

But let's consider a more concrete example. If one of the things you do regularly is transport your own and/or other children in a car pool, you probably place a high priority on having a car that's safe to drive. One day you take your car into your mechanic, who says that you need major repairs to keep the car going. It is no longer completely reliable.

Getting in Touch with What's Important to You

- What kinds of issues, needs, and activities really motivate me?
- If I could meet any need in the world, what would I do?
- Is there a group of people I am deeply concerned about?
- What needs and opportunities in my community do I feel strongly about?
- What kinds of people do I love to work with?
- Who are the people I most admire, and why? What do they do well that I might, too?

You may then decide, based on your priority of having a safe vehicle to drive, that your goal is to buy a new car.

Three Ways to Think About Your Priorities

The way I think about and establish priorities changes depending on what's going on in my life. I've used each of the following models over the years. Sometimes, especially when we're facing big changes, I've found it helps, over a short period of time, to use all of them. It's like the old tale about the blind men and the elephant: they all approached the elephant from different perspectives. One thought it was a big column; that person was feeling a leg. Another thought it was an animal similar to a snake. A third thought it was a big wall. You get the picture. Sometimes we need to look at something in a number of different ways to determine what it really is.

1. THE TOP-DOWN METHOD

One way to look at priorities is to try to determine what takes top priority in your life. Take a few minutes to think about what's in the top slot of your priority system. Here are some possibilities: financial security, a fulfilling marriage, a loving relationship with your children, peace of mind, good friends, social status, spiritual fulfillment, a loving extended family, interesting work, travel, education, fun and recreation, a great body, pretty clothes, a nice car, a beautiful home, recognition or fame, good health, longevity.

Now write your own list. Try to make the items as concrete as possible. Go over it and circle your top priority. Put your list away for a day or a week. Take it back out. Is the circled item still your top priority?

I'd say my top priority is having a fulfilling spiritual life. But that naturally involves other priorities, because as I grow in my spiritual life, I see the importance of a strong marriage and a happy family, of my own personal development, of my relationships with other people, of my work, of being financially responsible, of trying to help my kids grow emotionally, mentally, physically, and spiritually. The list keeps growing. So even when we've selected a top priority, we need to explore how our *sub-priorities*, if you will, lead us to living each day according to that top one.

Use your top priority list to arrange your sub-priorities under the top one. List the sub-priorities that are linked to your top priority.

2. THE WHAT-IF METHOD

What-iffing can be an exercise in futility and frustration if it's done in a way that slips over into "if only," as in "If only we had more money, a bigger house, more time together, I'd be happy." But what-if brainstorming can help you figure out and articulate priorities you've been vague about or didn't know you had. There are several ways of putting yourself in the what-if mode.

One good way is asking yourself, What if I won the lottery? What are ten things I would do? Why? How would the way I use my time and energy change? There are, of course, no right answers to these questions. The first thing you think of might be that you'd quit the job you hate. But then perhaps quitting your job might be at the end of your list, or not even on it at all. What would that mean to you? I think it could mean that you love your job, and that doing it well is probably a pretty high priority for you.

> "Any company (or any organization for that matter) needs a strong, unifying sense of direction. But that need is particularly strong in an organization in which tasks are differentiated and responsibilities are dispersed."
> —Christopher A. Bartlett

> "How we spend our days is, of course, how we spend our lives. There is no shortage of good days. It is good lives that are hard to come by."
> —Annie Dillard

Another good what-if question is, What if I had a year to live? How would I spend my time? What would I make sure I told my kids? My spouse? Where would I want to travel? How would I spend my money? Whom would I want to spend time with? Doing this exercise can be both exhilarating and sobering. If your answers are a lot different from how you work and live now, you might want to consider using them to rearrange your priorities.

3. THE ANY-TWO-OF-US-ARE-SMARTER-THAN-ANY-ONE-OF-US METHOD

This method involves nothing more than good old-fashioned talking. I recommend talking on a regular basis. Periodically Bill and I go out for an evening or a day together simply to discuss how we're spending our time and energy and money and what that says about what's important to us. No corporate manager or CEO operates alone, and I don't recommend it for Family Managers either. I don't think there's a marriage counselor in the world who would discourage couples from really talking with and listening to each other. Even if you're both on the same track as far as priorities for spending time and money go, when you spend time together you'll build closeness and think of inventive ways to live by your priorities. If you hold different priorities, talking about those priorities and looking for creative compromises that will meet both persons' needs can go a long way toward making your family life more peaceful and rewarding.

A few pages ago I talked about mistaking goals for priorities. Another common misconception about priorities is that they're never-changing. We set them, polish them up, and put them on a shelf, something like bowling trophies or fine China vases. At any rate, they're there and we

know what they are and that they'll always be there—should we ever decide
we need them. Not so. Children grow
older, jobs and situations change, and
so do priorities. A good way to get out of
touch with yourself, your spouse, and
your family is to continue living by yesterday's priorities. A periodic redoing of these
exercises can keep that from happening.

> "People who want to move mountains must start by carrying away small stones."
> —Anonymous

> "Tell me to what you pay attention, and I will tell you who you are."
> —José Ortega y Gasset

Living by Your Priorities

Remember the old maxim "Actions speak louder than words"? Well, it's
true. So far this chapter has been mostly about words, highfalutin ones
at that, as Aunt Mabel might have said.

What are our priorities? Are they ones we can reasonably act on? And
how *do* we act on them? We need to know what our priorities are to act
on them, but they're not really priorities *unless* we act on them.

I don't know what your priorities are, of course, but I imagine if
you're reading this book that pretty high on your list is making your
home a comfortable, happy, peaceful, and rewarding place. You may be
thinking I've been taking happy pills to even suggest that a mother with
two full-time careers can show her children that they are high on her
priority list when she has limited time. But on a recent weekend visit
with friends in Connecticut, I was with just such a mother. Cynthia is
the president of a successful marketing consulting business. She has a
babysitter at her home during the day and has given the sitter good and
specific directions concerning what she
wants to happen with her three-year-old
son. The babysitter also helps with housework and grocery shopping. Then when
Cynthia comes home, she is *really* home.

> We need to know what our priorities are to act on them, but they're not really priorities *unless* we act on them.

Having our priorities in place is like having a fancy new camera with an automatic focus feature and a built-in zoom lens. No more lost photo ops because we're fooling around with the shutter speed and the f-stop. When we look at life through the lens of our priorities, everything is in clear focus.

I heard her turn down invitations to fancy parties. She told me of declining new jobs that could bring in lots of money because they'd also take more time than she now spends at her office. She seldom turns on the TV at night. The time she spends with her three-year-old is indeed quality time—lots of reading, listening to tapes, playing together. Every night before he goes to bed Cynthia has the ritual of having her son recap his day for her. She shows intense interest in his world—the bugs he saw, the foods he liked and disliked, the people with whom he visited, what he learned, how he felt. She plans something fun to do with him every Saturday, and they go to church together every Sunday.

This is not to say that Cynthia doesn't do things for herself. She plays in a tennis league once a week—but they play from 9:00 to 10:00 P.M., after her son is fast asleep. She gets up early every morning and works out before he gets up. Once a week she gets a manicure on her lunch hour. She reads material she enjoys, not just what is required for her business. She plans to learn American sign language this year simply because she wants to. She's looking for a way to do this without taking time away from her child. But she wants to teach it to her son, too, so there's a bonus there.

The minutes of the day we have with our children come with a choice on how we'll spend them. You don't have to have a lot of money to spend great time with your kids. Going on field trips to state parks, walking the dog and talking about the day, baking cookies together on a rainy weekend afternoon, and reading a story together every night without fail—that's the stuff meaningful relationships are made of. The same is true for all other priorities: how we act in regard to them reveals how strongly we hold them.

Sometimes I think that Americans have lost their sense of being accountable for their time, in large part due to watching TV. Two hours can pass with nothing meaningful happening between family members. We have all sorts of excuses. We're too tired to do anything else. We simply must know what happened to the family on our favorite show. So every night in millions of households across the country the tube is on and the family is out of touch.

> "The best things in life aren't things." —Art Buchwald
>
> "With the appearance of the two-bathroom home, Americans forgot how to cooperate. With the appearance of the two-car family we forgot how to associate, and with the coming of the two-television home we forgot how to communicate."
> —Dr. John Baucom

Then we say, "I don't have the time to ____." You fill in the blank. Actually, I think most of us do have the time but just don't use it well, according to the priorities we say we embrace.

How We Spend Our Time Speaks Volumes

When business leaders set priorities, they think about those priorities in terms of the impact following them will make. For instance, companies that have a serious commitment to customer satisfaction set return policies and hours of operation and many more things that reflect that priority. As Family Managers, we live out our priorities in each of the seven departments, and how we spend our time in each department says a mouthful about what those priorities are. For example:

Time. Say you put a premium on spending time with your child. This means you don't raise your hand when your boss asks for volunteers to work at a food bank for an hour after work once a week because you've committed to take your child to the library for story hour. On the other hand, perhaps another of your priorities is teaching your child to show compassion for others. Perhaps you say yes to your boss after all and take your child with you.

Food. If eating well without spending hours every night in the kitchen while your kids get crankier and crankier is high on your priority list, you might invest in one of many good quick-meal cookbooks. Or you might enlist anybody who's big enough to hold a spoon in helping to cook and get dinner on the table, thereby spending time with your children and teaching them responsibility. If you use unbreakable dishes, which you probably do at least some of the time if you have small children, even a toddler can set the table. Or you might choose to spend time one weekend a month cooking in quantity and putting meals in the freezer.

Home and Property. Do you have an impressive magazine-cover-worthy family room filled with expensive furniture that everyone is afraid to touch, much less relax on? Or do you have attractive but comfortable and welcoming furniture that says, "Come on in and sit a while, prop up your feet, let your hair down, be refreshed?" It depends on your priorities.

Finances. Is it a higher priority to have a large nest egg in savings or to spend some of the money to add on a family rec room or go on a fabulous once-in-a-lifetime family vacation? How can you cut costs and still have a good vacation? Is anybody in your family a do-it-yourselfer? You? Your spouse? Your teenager, the one who got an A in shop? Could that person teach the rest of you a trick or two, and could you remodel for less money while spending time together as a family? I know from personal experience that you can build a bookcase in the time it takes to watch a made-for-TV movie.

Special Projects. If you prioritize honoring who each of your children is, then do you impose the birthday party you always wanted on your nine-year-old daughter? Or do you let her choose what she wants for herself? I have a friend who gave her daughter that very option. Within reason, her daughter could have any kind of birthday party she wanted. At first the daughter couldn't think of what she wanted. Then she had a flood of ideas—everything from a bowling party to a swimming party in a hotel pool (a treat for this winter birthday girl) to a less elaborate party to which she could invite every girl in her class. Her mother worked with her as she painstakingly outlined each idea on paper, thinking about whom to invite, what they would do, where the party might be. In the end, I think she had complete plans for at least five parties. Instead of discouraging her creativity, her mother talked with her about how much time they'd need to execute each different party, about how much each version would cost, and about how to weigh various options and make a decision. She chose to have a tea party for just a few close friends in their very best dress-up clothes at a Victorian bed and breakfast in their town. Not only did this girl get to make a choice on her own, thereby learning something about living by her priorities, she also learned a lot about making a plan and carrying it out. And she learned that her mother cared about her very much.

Family and Friends. If working on your marriage is a priority and spending more intimate moments together in the bedroom is one way you plan to do this, then you'll look at your calendar and figure out which nights during the week would be likely ones for a romantic rendezvous after the kids go to bed. You'll look for ways during the day to conserve some energy and think romantic thoughts to get ready.

Personal. Which is more valuable: to say yes, you'll work through your lunch hour on a project, or to say no because you have a prior commitment, and that commitment is to work out at a gym every day at noon?

> What we do, we do well. But we do not do it all.

Avoiding Traps

It's a good idea to live by priorities, perhaps you're thinking, *but I'm so busy I can't even take time to sort them out, let alone live by them.* Your obligations to your family, the office, and the community may seem overwhelming at times. You feel caught in a rapidly flowing river of daily demands with no paddle and no way to stop and see where you are going. All of us face numerous obstacles that keep us from setting priorities and ordering our lives the way we would like to. The big three that I fight in my own life are:

1. *Circumstances.* Unless we decide it's vitally important that we take an hour or so and go someplace quiet, where we can think about what's important to us, we face a life of minimal accomplishments, meaningless activities, frustration, and mediocrity.

2. *Expectations of and pressure from others.* We are all more or less prone to succumb to the agendas of others and compromise. For a long time I lived a life dominated by shoulds, ought tos, and musts, trying frantically to please everyone around me. I would drag myself out of bed in the morning and hurry through the day, crossing tasks off my list, meeting everyone's agenda but my own, never finishing all I had to do. Eventually, I reached crash-and-burnout and landed in the hospital with chronic fatigue syndrome. It was a costly way to learn I can't do it all, so I must do what's most important—to me and my family, that is. Peer pressure is not just a teenager's problem. It's a lifelong issue. And it's never too late to start standing on your own and supporting your priorities.

3. *Love of the comfortable.* We tend to arrange our lives as best we can to avoid pain and maintain our personal comfort. But significant change for the better, personal growth, and emotional development involve stepping out of the comfort zone. Change, even for something good like living by our priorities, is hard. It's easier to stay "as is." But if "as is" is not where you want to be or who you want to be or how you want to live your life, then maybe it's time to experience a little discomfort now for a long-term payoff. For example, a few years ago a wellness expert told me that over the course of our lives our metabolism slows down, some 10 percent a decade, and if we don't want to automatically gain weight as we age, we need to strength-train. Working out with weights builds muscle, not so we'll look like body builders, but so we'll be stronger and more able to resist gravity and the physical changes involved with aging. The problem is, strength training is painful—very painful. When I started working with weights, my muscles were really sore for a week or two, but I knew if I endured the short-term pain, I would get the long-term results that I wanted. This is a worthy exchange.

> "Change is not made without inconvenience, even from better to worse."
> —Samuel Johnson

Maybe your life is running out of control. You know you haven't been living by the priorities you want to. You know things have to change. What to do? You prioritize what's valuable to you. But you can't just do a few computer special effects to change things drastically immediately. You didn't get yourself where you are overnight, and things probably won't change overnight.

Are You Headed for Crash-and-Burnout?

Burnout Indicators
- Fatigue
- Insomnia
- Mental lapses
- Headaches
- Loss of sexual interest
- Irritability
- Rashes
- Ulcers
- Illness

You have to *synthesize*, which means to form something new by bringing together unrelated parts. Synthesizing doesn't mean totally changing everything (although there have been times when my house has been so out of control, moving sounded easier than reorganizing). It means weaving new ideas into the existing fabric of our lives. It means changing—sometimes slowly, other times abruptly—and looking for ways to incorporate new tactics, behaviors, and activities into our lives that will produce positive results. It's the opposite, in many ways, of throwing the baby out with the bathwater.

You have to start someplace. If you're having trouble beginning with the small pebbles to move the mountain, I suggest that you think about one day at a time. Get yourself a small notebook and write your top priorities in it. Then as you make choices during the day, simply jot down a few words about the choice you made and how it did or did not match your stated priorities. You're doing this not to beat yourself up for failing to make choices according to your priorities, but to become conscious of your actions. Maybe you'll find, as a friend of mine did, that she was trying to do too many things at once, and you'll decide to cut back. Or maybe you'll discover that something you thought was a priority because it always has been really isn't one anymore.

I used to put in a lot of overtime above and beyond my two full-time jobs. I said yes to everyone who asked me to volunteer for anything. I have no illusion that I am unique in that respect. Part of being a yea-sayer is cultural, I think. As women, we are likely to have been trained to please other people. And pleasing other people isn't necessarily bad—unless we do it at the expense of our families, our health, or our own goals and aspirations. The world will not stop spinning on its axis if we say "No, I can't" to an appeal for our time or energy.

> "If you know what you want to be and do, you must also know what you don't have to be and do."   —Anonymous

Another reason I think we say yes to so many requests is that we don't have a clear idea of our own priorities, of what we want for our own lives and for our families. Nature abhors a vacuum. If we don't know what we want, we likely will fill up all our available time with activities that might be good things but not necessarily what we want until there's no time to do the things most important to us.

> "Don't live your life based on what other people might think. You'll never make them or yourself happy."
> —Jean Brooks

> "In the end, what affects your life most deeply are things too simple to talk about."
> —Nell Blaine

Finally, because our culture tends to value measurable financial success above all other kinds, we tend to forget or diminish the importance of what we do as Family Managers. It's critical that we recognize the value of our job. You might not be able to see it in the Dow Jones average or this year's GNP, but I believe that every time we take time out to play a game with a grade schooler, to cut short a business meeting so we can have dinner together as a family, or to proofread a high schooler's personal essay on a college application, we are making a difference in the future of this country. Every positive thing you and I do for our husbands and our kids and ourselves, everything we do to make our homes a place where people grow toward their full potential, helps build strong families. Strong families build strong communities; strong communities build a strong culture; strong culture builds a strong country.

What to Keep on Your Calendar

When considering which activities to say yes to, many women are motivated by guilt. They think to themselves, *My mother always did this* or *Everyone else is doing it, so I guess I should, too.* Or maybe a pushy person makes a request we feel helpless to turn down. We each need to stop and consider how we are individually and uniquely wired before we say yes. The fact that something needs to be done

> Consider how you are individually and uniquely wired before you say yes to a request.

Saying "Yes" Means Saying "No"

Each of us has a limited amount of time, talent, and resources. So, in order to say "yes" to the things that are in harmony with our priorities, we must create the time and energy by saying "no" to other things.

is not enough reason to dedicate our time and energy to it. We must know if the activity is in harmony with our skills and priorities (or passions). When our skills (our talents and expertise) and our passions (those things or causes about which we feel strongly) are in sync with what we are doing, we will feel energized and will probably do a good job. When we are involved in things we are not skilled at and do not feel passionate about, we will feel drained of energy and will likely do no better than a mediocre job.

Evaluate the opportunities and activities in your life. If possible, delegate or say no to those that are not in harmony with who you are.

Basically, setting and keeping priorities makes you not only less harried but more fulfilled, because you're spending time and energy on the things that really matter to you. While I'm no longer Room Mother of the Year, I'm probably closer to being Mother of the Year in James's mind. And it's easy to say which is more important to me in the long run.

"Concentrate on the issues that are most important to you and minimize or ignore the nonessentials."
—James C. Nunan

ACTIVITY	AM I PASSIONATE ABOUT THIS?		WILL THIS ENERGIZE OR DRAIN ME?	WHO ELSE COULD DO THE ACTIVITY?
_____	❏Yes	❏No	_____	_____
_____	❏Yes	❏No	_____	_____
_____	❏Yes	❏No	_____	_____
_____	❏Yes	❏No	_____	_____
_____	❏Yes	❏No	_____	_____
_____	❏Yes	❏No	_____	_____
_____	❏Yes	❏No	_____	_____
_____	❏Yes	❏No	_____	_____
_____	❏Yes	❏No	_____	_____
_____	❏Yes	❏No	_____	_____
_____	❏Yes	❏No	_____	_____
_____	❏Yes	❏No	_____	_____

Keeping Your Balance

- Pat yourself on the back for a relationship or situation in which you've made a good trade-off.
- Make sure your "god" is worthy of your worship.
- Filter information, don't just accept it.
- Let your priorities help you see the forest when you're lost in the trees.
- Remind yourself that the proof of the priority is the action you take on it.
- Choose to endure short-term pain for a long-term payoff.

FOUR
Live in Two Tenses

"Effective managers live in the present—but concentrate on the
future."   —James L. Hayes

You read that title right: live in two tenses, the present and the
future. It is easier to choose one or the other than to try to live
in both. But if I do that, I rob myself and my family. There are
various ways of living in the future, and I used to be an expert at the
kind that isn't very useful. It goes something like this: when the kids
are older—out of braces and out of college—and we live in a bigger
house—one that's completely organized and easy to take care of—and
we've paid off the mortgage and have plenty of money in the bank, then
I'll take time to relearn to play the piano, work out regularly, take a
dance class, get my master's degree, and take a trip with girlfriends for
no reason other than to have fun and enjoy each other's company. That
perfect future was right around the corner. I was sure of it. All I had to
do was be patient and it would come.

On the other hand, I've also had experience living in the present to
the extent that I failed to take time and energy to dream and envision
great things for my family and myself; therefore they never happened.
"Be prepared" is the Boy Scout motto, and it's not a bad motto for anybody, Family Managers included. One big thing my husband and I prepared for recently was having two sons in college at once. We knew for

"Time is the scarcest resource, and unless it is managed nothing else can be managed." —Peter Drucker

a long time we had to plan ahead for the financial impact, including helping our sons think about part-time jobs and financial aid. But I also had to think about how the changes would affect our family life. Bill and I had to get used to having kids who don't live at home, to honor their new status as "almost adults," to let them go, and at the same time, to continue a parental relationship with them. We began talking about college six years ago when John, our oldest, was just starting to think about which ones to apply to, and now the future is here. In order to function effectively, meeting today's demands and providing for tomorrow's dreams and needs, I had to be able to live in both tenses.

When I began applying the management principles I learned in business to home and work, I began to see that I could make better decisions about each day if I was continuously aware of what the future might bring. It's a paradox, but living in two tenses made me more aware of the present moment. For instance, while John was getting ready to go to college, I was also consciously spending as much quality time with him as I could, storing up memories against the time when he'd be away from home.

Living in the future does not mean putting things off until tomorrow, and living in the present doesn't mean we don't plan for the future. It's as simple as that.

Mystery Men and Space Cadets

Living in the present has everything to do with paying attention and showing up fully prepared at the right time. Living in the future means thinking ahead about what you want to happen and ensuring that the right actions will take place at the right time and will include the right people with the right equipment so your goals will be met. Whether it's getting your family out the door—shoes tied, zippers zipped, faces

free of grape-juice stains—for your cousin's wedding or researching what you'll
need to do to your house to have it
ready to put on the market when summer

> You have to consciously work on today and tomorrow at the same time.

comes, you have to consciously work on today and tomorrow at the
same time.

Doing that requires two different sets of skills. And, in my experience, people tend to be better at one than the other. It's like being
right- or left-handed. You just are. On the other hand, I've found over
and over again that men who practice living in two tenses in their
careers are often not experienced in doing the same thing when it
comes to running a home. In matters of Family Management, men just
don't live in both tenses the way they do in their business world. They
do perfectly well living in the present and the future when planning
budgets and growth and using market trends and predictions to make
decisions. Some might even understand two-tense living when it comes
to something they're particularly interested in, like getting ready for a
fishing trip or remodeling the family room. But look for that same
thought combined with action when it comes to doing weekly household chores, making or keeping appointments, or getting a kid to his
after-school activities, and often you'll look in vain. At least that's my
experience.

In our household, for example, Tuesdays and Fridays are the busiest
mornings of the week, and have been for quite a while. Typically, a
Tuesday at the Peels' house runs like this: I set my alarm a little earlier
so I'll still have time to work out and go to the grocery store before tackling the other demands of the day. I hurry through my exercise routine
and gather the needed groceries before heading home to see if by
chance the garbage, which is always collected on Tuesday, has miraculously been deposited in the big cans outside. No such luck. When I
enter the house, I am met by the aroma of overripe garbage waiting to
go out and the snores of my mate.

Humming "Alone Again, Naturally," I rush through the house, emptying trash containers while planning what I will pack for James's lunch. I also scan each closet, since no one else has remembered Tuesday is also D-day: Dry-cleaning Day. Checking to see that James is conscious and moving, I make sure he's remembered to lay out his Boy Scout uniform and materials, as well as his tennis shorts and racquet. Then I dash to the kitchen to start breakfast and wait for the guys to appear.

And they do, looking innocent, hungry, and (annoyingly) well rested. Bill sits down, starts reading the paper, then looks up at me and asks, "Why do you have that look on your face?"

So I tell him again how I've been running around for almost three hours living in the future, my mind focused on the next task. It's not that Bill doesn't take equal responsibility for chores around the house. It's that I'm always the advance person, the one who keeps things moving ahead. He just doesn't think of the myriad tasks that have to be done before something at which he shows up can be enjoyed. (Vacations, and all that has to happen before we set off, are another example.)

To be fair to my spouse, though, I do need to go back to the idea of one person not being equally good at both living in the future and the present, whether it's at home or in the office. My family knows that I can be a bit of a space cadet. I have tried to write a to-do list while driving on the freeway—not something I recommend! Sometimes I live so much in the future that the present day passes in a blur, and I forget what I'm doing because I'm thinking about what needs to be done next Saturday. This can have consequences, especially when I'm cooking. More than a few times I have let the pasta pot boil dry. Do you have any idea what that smells like? And how hard it is to clean the pan? Or I'll be so busy thinking about the next section on a writing project that I'll forget where I put the files for the last in the computer storage system and what I named them. Bill has had to come to my rescue more than once by finding the latest version of Chapter 1, which I had given the file name "Chapter 5" because I was working on the fifth version of it.

The point I'm making is to accept each other and patiently help our mates with lists and gentle reminders of what needs to be done.

Being Present in the Present

First of all, we must live deliberately in the present. We must be aware of the way we spend not only our work hours but also our leisure hours—resting the mind or stimulating it (both are important), doing nothing or everything (both are destructive), working for things in the future or worrying about the past. For the dual-career woman particularly, even five-minute segments are important; only ten of them add up to almost an hour. What do you do with those segments?

> "Know the true value of time; snatch, seize, and enjoy every moment of it. No idleness; no laziness, no procrastination: never put off till tomorrow what you can do today."
> —Philip Dormer Stanhope

> "Seize this very minute. What you do or dream, you can begin it."   —Goethe

> "We think in generalities, but we live in detail."
> —Alfred North Whitehead

For years I felt frustrated, always behind, never accomplishing what I thought I needed or wanted to. I had a list of things to do, but I was waiting for large blocks of time to accomplish them in. For instance, I'd say to myself, "When I've got half a day, I'll clean out all the drawers and closets and organize the kitchen cabinets or the kids' toys." The time never came. Now I realize that very few of us are lucky enough to have large blocks of time. The present happens in minute increments.

When I got the idea to break down those large blocks into five-minute segments, it changed my life. Now I accomplish a lot more because I see five-minute segments as gold and as a way to get some portion of a task behind me. Maybe I'll start by cleaning out one bathroom drawer or half the silverware drawer. I can do the other half when I see another five minutes. The same goes with decluttering my closet. In five minutes I can cull out the blouses I don't wear anymore.

Then later I can grab five minutes to work on the skirts, and so on. A little present time here and a little there, and finally I've finished something.

As a home-based writer with magazine and book deadlines one after the other, I've learned to work on a paragraph for five minutes, then answer a phone call from James's school, then e-mail my editor an idea for a chapter, then write another paragraph, then answer another phone call from a newspaper, then fax the information the reporter needs, then answer the door and show the electrician where the breaker box is located, then write another paragraph, and so on— five minutes at a time. If I waited for large blocks of time to write

The Great Time Thief

We sometimes want to put off distasteful chores—present and future ones. Procrastinating robs us of valuable time. To fight procrastination try these ideas.

- Set a firm day and time to tackle an unpleasant task. Note the date and project on your calendar, as you would any other appointment.
- Write down the steps you need to take to finish a job. List tasks in the order you should perform them—then check off each step as you complete it so you can see your progress.
- Break up distasteful jobs into small pieces. Grit your teeth and work at the job for short stretches of time. Before you know it, you'll be on the road to finishing.
- Be accountable to a friend or coworker. Tell someone about your task and your time limit. Report back when you're finished.
- Create mini-completions within a long-term project. For example, if you're overseeing the yearlong effort to raise funds for school computers, establish interim completion points. Reward yourself each time you raise enough money for one terminal.
- Try the "carrot" approach. After you've finished an unpleasant task, reward yourself. Take a coffee break or a walk. Or allow yourself to spend an equal amount of time working on a favorite project.

what I've committed to write, the ink would never meet the paper and I'd be out of a job.

Figuring out the way you use all of your time will help you discover wasted minutes or hours that you can use more effectively. If you're a dual-career woman, you probably know that every moment you're not in the office is golden. I'm also betting that the same time-saving and scheduling techniques that you use at your office can be employed in your job as Family Manager.

Get your family thinking about how

"Funny how we get so exact about time at the end of life and at its beginning. She died at 6:08 or 3:46, we say, or the baby was born at 4:02. But in between we slosh through huge swatches of time—weeks, months, years, decades even."
—Sister Helen Prejean

"I would I could stand on a busy corner, hat in hand, and beg people to throw me all their wasted hours."
—Bernard Berenson

Track Your Time

If you're skeptical about finding even five-minute blocks of extra time in your life, try this exercise. Keep a journal that reflects how your time is divided during a typical day or two plus one weekend day. Record what you do and how long you spend doing it, from morning to night, in thirty-minute increments. Be sure to include the following:

- What time you get out of bed
- What you do while commuting to and from work
- How long it takes to complete small tasks and large projects
- Phone calls—how many, how long, and what they're about
- Shopping and errands—when you go and how long it takes
- Length of breaks (including lunch)
- When and how long you watch TV
- When and how long you clean house, cook, and do laundry
- What or who interrupts you
- How much time you spend searching for misplaced items
- What and how long you read

Ten 5-Minute Present-Tense Tasks

- Clean off a refrigerator shelf.
- Repot a plant.
- Clean the sink.
- Write a thank-you note.
- Put in a load of laundry.
- Organize your sweater drawer.
- Dust the living room.
- Pay a few bills.
- Return three phone calls. (If you have only five minutes you won't be tempted to spend time in idle chatter.)
- Tell your kids and/or husband how much you appreciate them.

they can help if they have an extra five minutes. Make a list of quick tasks and post it so they can refer to it easily. Here are some ideas to get you started:

- Unload the dishwasher.
- Sort a load of clean socks.
- Set the table.
- Program the VCR to record a show.
- Sew on a button.
- Vacuum a room.
- Brush the dog or cat.
- Strip a bed and take linens to the laundry room.
- Sweep the porch.
- Pick up clutter.

Staying out from under the Pile

In my efforts to efficiently live in the present, to control—not be controlled by—the daily needs and demands of my family and career, and

Ten 5-Minute Future-Tense Tasks

- Make doctor's and dentist's appointments.
- Write a to-do list for the day or the week.
- Phone to get a vacation brochure or make reservations.
- Plan a date with your husband and secure a babysitter for Saturday night.
- Call the bakery to order a cake for your child's class picnic.
- Buy the perfect gift for your sister's birthday when you see it, even if her birthday isn't for six months.
- Plan next week's menus.
- Jot down your personal goals for the next six months.
- Read over your previously written goals for the time you're going through now and do a quick evaluation.
- Coordinate business and family calendars with your husband.

to plan ahead effectively, I created a list that allows me to track details for each of the seven Family Management departments. I call it a Hit List. It helps because it:

1. Declutters our minds by providing a systematic way to sort through the myriad chores and responsibilities that crowd in every day.
2. Clears our perspective, revealing what's trivial and what's priority.
3. Clarifies which tasks only we can do and which can be delegated or shared.
4. Improves our memory through the exercise of writing details down.
5. Helps us remember what steps to take today so that whatever's coming tomorrow will be smooth.

Here is an example of my Hit List.

FAMILY MANAGER HIT LIST

Home and Property	Food	Family and Friends	Finances
Special Projects	Time and Scheduling	Personal	Other Job

Date _____

As you begin to use this Hit List, accept the reality that you won't always be able to check off all the tasks on your list at the end of the day. Don't be discouraged by this! Move unaccomplished tasks to the next day's list, or delete the ones you deem unimportant for now. Use the Hit List as an opportunity for improvement rather than discouragement, as an occasion for celebrating all you *did* get done. If you don't become an expert in a week or two, don't despair. This list is for women who are desperately busy, and desperately busy women don't become

> "Finish every day and be done with it. You have done what you could. Some blunders and absurdities no doubt crept in; forget them as soon as you can. Tomorrow is a new day. Begin it well."
> —Ralph Waldo Emerson
>
> "Where there's a will there's a way." —Proverb
>
> "Every moment spent planning saves three or four in execution."
> —Crawford Greenwalt

perfect via planning. They just get better and better, and that has far-reaching effects on their families and their jobs.

The Future Tense

In their book *Mission Possible*, Ken Blanchard and Terry Waghorn suggest that companies who want to stay on the cutting edge of progress must learn to think futuristically—to foretell the future. Of course nothing is ever absolutely certain. That old adage "The road to the future is paved with uncertainty" has a great deal of truth to it. So does thinking futuristically mean palm reading or paying serious attention to fortune cookies? Of course not. Thinking futuristically means using a technique that companies call scenario planning. As Family Managers, we are regularly involved in scenario planning in three ways:

1. *Contingency planning.* Contingencies are not plans per se. They're hypothetical versions of what could possibly happen in the future. In Family Management, contingencies are what could happen in your family's future: the immediate future—tomorrow or the next

> "Everything comes to he that hustles while he waits."
> —Thomas Edison

day—as well as the distant future—a month, a year, or five years from now. To get a feel for contingency planning, imagine taking your family fishing at a lake next weekend. Suppose for a moment that you're ready to pile into the minivan with fishing poles and bait. To get to that point requires some minimal planning. You have to look at the map to see exactly which roads to take to get to the lake. Detailed though it may be, your map does little to prepare you for what lies ahead. It provides you with no information about such elements as weather, the availability of bathrooms, insects indigenous to the area, parks that might be closed for grounds maintenance, unruly neighbors, unfriendly wildlife, or facilities to eat in. To deal with these possibilities, you consider a limited number of what-if scenarios. What will you do if your child falls into the lake and gets soaking wet? What will you do if a thunderstorm comes up suddenly while you're in a rowboat in the middle of the lake? What if you chance upon a water moccasin? None of these events may occur, but any might. To be adequately prepared, you have to contingency-plan.

For a Family Manager with the double responsibilities of family and career, learning to contingency-plan can mean the difference between chaos and calm. What if on the morning of your big presentation, which is scheduled for eight-thirty, your daughter remembers she has to have a special notebook from the office supply store that doesn't open until eight? What if while you are in a meeting you get a call from your child's day care center that your preschooler has a fever? What if your used car finally refuses to be used anymore? What if your daughter plans to attend not just college, but medical school? What if you or your spouse has to retire early? This is where the word *contingency* comes to mean volumes in the mind and life of a good Family Manager. This is about living in two tenses, in the present while planning for the future.

Planning for contingencies in every department can relieve stress and save time. For example, always have an emergency set of clean clothes for your child put away for that day when you have to go someplace and you haven't

> "Forethought and prudence are the proper qualities of a leader."   —Tacitus

had a chance to do laundry; alternative meals for when you have to stay late at work and don't have time to fix the fajitas you'd planned on; money set aside in a special account for emergencies; gifts put away on your closet shelf when your friend's (or your child's friend's) birthday is (whoops!) today and you had forgotten or your child tells you an hour before a birthday party; a friend or two who can pick up your son or daughter if he or she gets sick suddenly while you're tied up at work.

2. *Advance work.* Another way you scenario-plan is to look ahead at what's coming up on your family's calendar and think through the steps you need to take for the event to happen à la best-case scenario.

We have a friend who used to be one of President Bush's advance men. He would go into a city a few days before Bush and make sure all the details were taken care of so the president would have a smooth, trouble-free visit to that city. As Family Managers, we act as advance men for small and large family events. Something as simple as a date with your husband next weekend takes some advance work. You need to collect information: What time will you both get home from work? What kind of food are you in the mood for? Do you want to go to a movie? If so, is there one you'd both like to see and what time does it start? Then you decide who will be responsible for securing a babysitter, what the kids will eat for dinner that night, and what they'll do. You may also think about making dinner reservations and picking up tickets early if the film you want to see is just opening or quite popular.

Taking a great family vacation next summer takes a lot of advance work that you and your family can enjoy doing together: collecting information from the places you'd like to go, creating a vacation budget, researching accommodations and transportation costs, collecting and/or buying any needed clothes or gear, making kennel reservations for pets, getting your car trip-ready if you're driving, packing, asking the mail carrier to hold your mail, telling your neighbors how long you'll be gone and where you can be reached.

3. *Telling the story.* When cutting-edge companies plan to launch a new product, they know how important it is for everybody from accounting to manufacturing to marketing to buy into the plan. They also know that success is in the details. So they call together key team members who plan by writing the scenario—telling the story of what will happen in all areas of the company as the new product is launched. What extra resources will be needed in research and development? In marketing? In shipping?

As Family Managers, we don't usually launch new products, but we can scenario-plan to make our dreams come true. What did you write on your Dream List in Chapter 2? What are the possible scenarios there? Are you, for example, planning to remodel your kitchen or your bathroom, well-known stress-producing projects where lots can go wrong?

You no doubt meet as a family more than once to plan this major undertaking. You talk about what you all want and need in the rooms. You look at plans and at possible materials. You set deadlines and budgets. You decide what you're going to contract out and what you're going to do yourselves. Your daughters might suggest putting two sinks in the bathroom so they can share. Your son the basketball star may want higher counters in the kitchen. You might decide not to do that because it would be more expensive and wouldn't work for your seven-year-old, but you suggest some kind of a higher-than-standard freestanding butcher block unit so he can make his famous sub sandwiches comfortably.

As the project progresses, keep a record of all your meetings and ideas in a notebook, along with a file for color samples, quotes, and records of last-minute changes.

The bottom line: Scenario planning is the strategy of how you get from where you are now to where you want to be. It's envisioning what you want the future to hold, whether you're dreaming about best-case scenarios or

> "A good plan today is better than a perfect plan tomorrow."
> —General George S. Patton

simply getting prepared for the what-ifs. It's living in two tenses—the present and the future.

I recently read that one thing cutting-edge companies seem to have

Think Future Tense

- Start collecting information and putting aside money each month for that cruise you want to take for your tenth anniversary three years from now.
- Mark your calendar one month before holidays and family birthdays. Begin working on celebration plans early, buying presents and/or decorations.
- Keep take-out menus at work so you can order before you leave and pick up on the way home.
- When you make an appointment, write down the person's phone number on your calendar so you won't have to search if plans change.
- When you have a doctor's appointment, call ahead to see if he or she is on schedule.
- If you have small children, keep your car stocked with a diaper bag, a roll of paper towels, a change of clothes for the kids, and plastic containers filled with snacks.
- Schedule a time in the summer to have photos taken of your kids. Have one enlarged to give Grandma and Grandpa for Christmas.
- Start making summer vacation plans in March.
- Look at your calendar at the first of each month and secure babysitters for evenings you know you'll be out that month.
- Decide in November what you'll wear to holiday parties. Take care of drycleaning and mending now.
- Keep a change of clothes and/or accessories at the office for unexpected meetings or dinner engagements. (The probability of this happening increases on the days you wear jeans to work to clean your desk and bookshelves.)

in common is that they no longer relegate planning to once-a-year meet-ings in which a bunch of people sit around a conference table talking about five years down the road. Planning in these companies is a 365-day-a-year task that involves everyone. People think about where they are now and consider many future scenarios, some of them for to-morrow and some of them for ten years from now.

Living in the present and the future will help you do the same and keep your family balanced as you move ahead steadily, well prepared and confident. And you add to your lives the considerable pleasure of seeing your desires fulfilled, not just dreamed about.

Keeping Your Balance

- You can plan each day better if you are continually aware of what the future might bring.
- Two-tense living doesn't necessarily come naturally to both spouses.
- Five-minute segments are gold. Use them.
- Creating a Hit List is the first step in organizing all of the demands of today and tomorrow.
- Scenario planning can make the difference between chaos and calm.
- Planning is not a weekly, monthly, or annual event; it's daily.

FIVE
A Team That Works for All of You

"A workforce is willing to go through many painful things if it believes in the long-term goals." —Richard Belous

B ill and I have been talking about learning to sail. One of our long-term goals is to have a sailboat, but right now we're just at the dreaming-about-it stage. I've been reading magazines with lots of terms and techniques I'm not familiar with. One of the terms, *triangulation,* has turned out to have implications for Family Management.

Triangulation is a time-honored form of navigation. It's simple and effective. You can locate an unknown point by forming a triangle with two known points and the unknown point as vertices. If you know where the two points are, and you're making a triangle, there's only one place the third can be. The key is starting with two known points. Then you can find the third.

Imagine that the area of the triangle illustrated below represents any project or task you want it to represent. For example, say it's the weekly housecleaning you and your family have agreed to. The expectation, or destination, has been defined: the house will be cleaned once a week. But you don't know how you're going to get there. There are a lot of ways the house could get cleaned once a week. One possible way is that you, the Family Manager, could do it by yourself. Another possibility is hiring a housekeeper.

Figure 1

(Once these two are in place you can move to your destination or expectation—that the house will be cleaned once a week.)

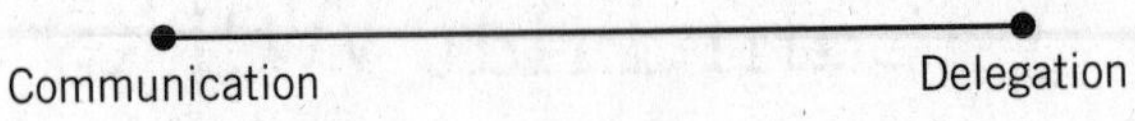

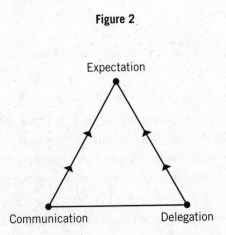

Figure 2

Or (my favorite!) you can communicate with each other, delegate responsibilities to each member of the family old enough to hold a dust cloth and not try to eat it, and reach your expectations.

Yes, there are housekeeping chores a toddler can do. I know one woman whose daughter helped clean the bathroom from the time she was about two and a half. The kid loved to play in water and be near her mom. So the mom bought some nontoxic cleanser—not a bad idea no matter *who's* doing the cleaning—and let her toddler clean out the bathtub. My kids feel lucky I didn't hear that story when they were young. They didn't have to clean the bathtub at an early age, but they did clean the baseboards and fronts of kitchen cabinets. I simply put socks over their hands and they wiped away. No, this really didn't help very much, but it taught them that they were members of the Peel Family Clean Team, and it set the stage for their accepting more difficult chores as they could handle them.

> "In order that people be happy in their work, these three things are needed: They must be fit for it; They must not do too much of it; And they must have a sense of success in it." —John Ruskin

Once you've determined your method through communication—ours is to work together as a team—then you have to delegate appropriately to each family member. This requires the third vertex of the triangle, expectation. You'll have to discuss exactly what needs to be done. Who's willing to do what? Who's good at doing what? Who's going to be in charge of making sure there are supplies? Who will see that expectations are met?

As you communicate and delegate, you may need to recommunicate (or renegotiate) your expectations. Maybe your idea of a clean living room is that everything is put away, pillows are fluffed, carpets are vacuumed, magazines are stacked nicely, and there are fresh flowers in a vase on the end table. Maybe your ten-year-old's idea is that he spends an hour cleaning underneath the sofa pillows (looking for coins and treasures) and vacuuming the center of the room, tending to ignore the fur balls under the coffee table and all the rest of the mess.

The point in navigation is to move from one place to another. The point in getting a project done is pretty much the same. And if you are clear on any two of the three points of the triangle, you'll find the third. But sometimes unexpected problems arise. There can be problems in communication or delegation. For example, you may think you told everyone that next Saturday was going to be a big yard-work day, but your teenager didn't register that and made plans to go out with friends instead. Then you've got something that looks like this:

Figure 3

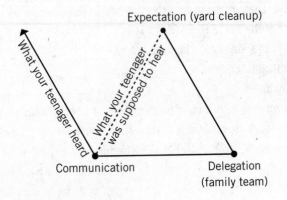

Communication takes a left turn, and you no longer have intersecting lines that get you to your expectation: a clean yard.

In this chapter, we're going to discuss strategies to bring communication, delegation, and expectations into the same triangle so that you're working together as a task force to do just about anything you as a family want to. I find, and I think you will too, that I learn a lot when we embark on new endeavors as a family.

If at First You Don't Get Where You Want to Be . . .

A few years ago, Bill and I decided to share the same home-office space. It made sense—on paper. We could spare ourselves the expense of double rent and two sets of office equipment. We would be in the same place at the same time when projects called for our joint input. We could balance our parenting and

> "I think housework is the reason most women go to the office." —Heloise
>
> "All life is an experiment."
> —Oliver Wendell Holmes, Jr.

earning-income responsibilities. When one parent was out of town or pushing to meet a deadline, the other could cover the kids and the household tasks. Our arrangement seemed perfect.

Reality was a rude awakening. All the loving feelings we enjoyed when we worked in separate spaces seemed to evaporate overnight. Heavy sighs, tight lips, and the occasional just-loud-enough-to-know-it-was-aimed-at-you grumbling became commonplace. Before, we had quiet when we were writing. Our environments, physical and electronic, were under our individual control.

Suddenly neither of us had control. We had to listen to each other's phone calls, muttering, conversations with people who came to the office, and swearing at the computer when a file disappeared. Our equipment strained under the demands of our separate publishers and media people's requests to print something out and fax it now . . . always *now*. I expected Bill to know when I needed silence. He expected me to cheer him up when he was stressed. I expected him to understand the importance of ambiance, which meant the office had to be cute. This was difficult when his side usually looked like an explosion had just occurred. Worst of all, Bill expected me to understand his work and make my top priority helping him, and I expected the same of him. It wasn't long before the question arose: Can a loving, understanding couple turn into a two-headed monster that devours itself and its young?

We think the answer is probably yes. There were times when if one of our unsuspecting offspring had wandered into the office with some unreasonable request (like "It's 7:00 P.M. Are we having dinner tonight?") we might have snapped him in two. So before we ended up in the emergency room or divorce court, we decided we had to make some changes.

When we combined offices, we believed that sharing an office would save us money, increase our creativity on projects we worked on together, and enable

> "There is no failure except in no longer trying."
> —Elbert Hubbard

us to be flexible in meeting the demands of our growing-up, needing-attention, needing-to-be-places sons. These expectations not only seemed reasonable and mutually beneficial, they actually were. The problem was, we weren't clear on where the other two points on the triangle were. Despite having been married twenty-plus years and knowing the benefits of communication, we hadn't hammered out the details. We hadn't agreed about who was in charge of what. Our wildly divergent ideas concerning who was doing what and how to talk about it was going to result in meltdown unless we did something quick.

When we don't meet each other's expectations, tension mounts. Tempers flare. Words fly—and wound—like darts. Fortunately, we have learned something over the years. It takes us a while, but we finally calm down, get smart, and talk about the issues beneath the tension. Inevitably it comes down to assumed expectations.

The way I saw it, Bill was choosing to place my desire for beauty and ambiance in a file marked "Low Priority." Thoughts began to swirl: *What's important to me is not important to him; therefore I'm not important. Why are his desires more worthy than mine? Hey, don't I help pay the mortgage on this office?* And so forth and so forth until the air was thick with tension. When he looked at me the wrong way one day, my eyes filled up and I blurted out the assumptions simmering just below the surface: "It's rude for you not to take into consideration the feelings of someone you share something with—especially your wife! You're acting like you're the only one in the room."

The way Bill saw it, I was totally absorbed in my own world and didn't care about what really mattered—finishing assignments, not creating atmosphere. His response to my outburst revealed his side: "Your work space and needs are not the only ones that are important. You act like they are. [Hmmm . . . that sounded familiar.] You expect me to drop everything I'm doing to rescue lost files, untangle the paper in the fax machine, and hang a pretty poster on the wall. What about my work? I need your help."

If the beginning of peace starts with the end of war, we were on our way, even with this heated discussion. Over time, our office became less a battleground and more a site for peaceful negotiation. We had to learn to express our expectations to each other and then be willing to bend a little in meeting them. We both had to take responsibility for making our workplace conducive to productivity, and we had to work at remaining relaxed and flexible. This had to be, like our marriage, a joint effort. So when I tell Bill I'll use another room for meeting with a reporter when he's laboring under a deadline, I do it. If he needs some room for brainstorming with colleagues, I'll arrange to do some activity other than writing at my desk during that time.

Once again, on paper, this sounds reasonable. And it's true: peace and stability reigned . . . for a time. Our office ran smoothly until the inevitable schedule clashes, mismatched deadlines and workloads, multiple kid responsibilities, and demands from the outside world impinged upon our carefully constructed system. We quickly learned that when change comes and demands a shift, we have two options. We can get angry because once again our expectations are not being met and we feel the other person is letting us down. We can express our frustration verbally or physically and the effect is the same: bad working conditions and no work getting done. Or we can move more quickly to the step we'll have to take eventually anyway: communication. We have to acknowledge that things have changed. We need to renegotiate.

Our years of experience in ironing out home and workplace wrinkles have given us a strategy for this and other touchy but necessary discussions.

1. Identify the issue or conflict area.
2. Attack the problem, not the person.
3. Bring an other-centered attitude to the negotiating table. Discover the joys of putting others before yourself.

> "When ideas fail, words come in very handy."　　—Goethe

> "Habit breaking, the prerequisite for change and renewal, needs more than a simple decision. It takes motivation, desire and will. Crisis can provide that and all too often is the sole force for change."
>
> —Robert H. Waterman

4. Listen to what the other person is saying and not saying.
5. Agree on a plan of action.
6. Test the plan.
7. Reinforce progress. ("Bill, I really appreciate your not using the speaker phone when I'm writing." "Kathy, thanks for having your meeting with Nancy in the other room. I was able to make my deadline.")
8. Reevaluate and negotiate as needed, which in our case is often.

Expectations

Sure, some women try to do it all alone. You may be, like I was once upon a time, bound and determined to be Supermom, Queen of Cuisine, and Ms. Better Homemaker, as well as Corporate Connie. It simply didn't work for me. I made myself and my family miserable with preconceived notions about how my house and my family should look and run. Notice those singular, first-person possessive pronouns: my, my, my. That was part of the problem. I wanted my home life to run my way, despite the fact that I didn't have the resources to pull it off alone, despite the fact—hindsight is so much more acute than foresight—that others lived in that house and that they had every right to their own ideas.

Some women want to do it their own way because that's what they've been trained to do. Some women base their self-esteem on being able to say, "I ironed all the shirts, cleaned the house, earned the bread and baked it." That's fine, I guess, if they aren't exhausted, if their family isn't suffering, and if they're not playing the role of the martyr in their family soap opera.

It's a well-known business principle that workers who buy into the company's goals are more likely to work to meet those goals. And one sure way to make sure they do is to see that they have a hand in setting those goals.

So start with expectations. What do you—that would be the plural you, everyone in your family who can talk—want in everything from relationships to, say, eating dinner together most nights a week? Or keeping everyone in clean clothes? You get the picture.

If you approach your family with the notion of teamwork and it's a hard sell, consider the idea that your family hears you saying you just want help doing things your way, meeting your expectations. If this is so, you will have to rethink your wants and your ways. What are your husband's goals? Your children's? How could working together as a team help each of you meet your individual goals? Find ways to mesh individual expectations with the family goal of an efficiently running home. Then it will be something that everyone is willing to work toward. For example, "After you wash a load of towels today, then we'll shop for a bookcase for your trophies."

> "Govern a family as you would cook a small fish: very gently."   —Chinese proverb

> "Communication is not just words, paint on canvas, math symbols or the equations and models of scientists; it is the interrelation of human beings trying to escape loneliness, trying to share experience, trying to implant ideas."
> —William M. Marstellar

> "Marriage is not just spiritual communion and passionate embraces; marriage is also three meals a day, sharing the workload and remembering to carry out the trash."
> —Dr. Joyce Brothers

Communication

In our family, keeping the peace starts with keeping all communication lines open. An unspoken expectation is an impossible expectation. And unwise delegations will be made unless everybody gets a say.

> An unspoken expectation is an impossible expectation.

If Bill and I had been able to com-

How Kids Can Help

Preschoolers can:

- Make their beds (use comforters for easier handling and cleaning).
- Fold towels and washcloths.
- Put away clothes in drawers.
- Pick up toys.
- Wipe off the front of large appliances using a spray bottle of water and sponge.
- Feed pets.
- Match clean socks.
- Scrub vegetables.

Kindergartners can do all of the above and:

- Vacuum small areas with a lightweight, handheld vacuum.
- Sweep porch.
- Straighten plastic dishes in a lower cabinet.
- Dust furniture.
- Wipe windows (that you've washed) with a clean blackboard eraser to keep them shining.

Younger elementary kids can do all of the above and:

- Take out garbage.
- Sweep stairs and walks.
- Clean out the car.
- Vacuum their own rooms.
- Sort and straighten toys.
- Empty the dishwasher.
- Sort clothes for washing.
- Clean off outdoor furniture.
- Water a garden.
- Set and clear the table.

Older elementary kids can do all of the above and:

- Clean bathroom mirrors.
- Vacuum most rooms.

- Clean toilets.
- Clean countertops and the kitchen sink.
- Mop small-area floors.
- Fold most laundry and put it away.
- Pull weeds.
- Clean pet areas.
- Put away groceries.
- Pack their own school lunches.
- Rake leaves.

Middle school kids can do all of the above and:
- Wash windows.
- Mend clothes.
- Mow yard.
- Wash car.
- Change sheets on beds.
- Do their own laundry.
- Clean the bathtub.
- Shovel snow.

High school kids can do all of the above and:
- Clean out refrigerator.
- Defrost freezer.
- Clean out and organize attic, basement, garage.
- Do heavy yard work.
- Clean light fixtures.
- Wax the car.
- Learn to repair and maintain the car.
- Fix dinner

municate earlier and more clearly, we might have staved off some of the adjustment period involved in learning to share our office. On the other hand, some miscommunications, wrangling, and readjustments are inevitable.

Family Management, like all other good management, is not about autocratic leaders imposing arbitrary standards from on high. It's about sharing responsibility, helping each person find his or her niche, and empowering each to succeed. Everyone gets a say.

Sometimes what is said will raise concerns. There are a lot of similarities between a company and a family, one of which is the fact that when they are faced with the possibility of change, people of any age express similar anxieties. They want to know:

- What the changes will mean and what is wrong with the way things are now.
- How the changes will affect them personally, what's in it for them, how they will find the time, and if they will have the skills to implement the changes.
- What they should do first, second, third. How they will manage the details. How long it will take.
- Will the effort be worth it? Will the change make a difference? Will it pay off?
- Who else will be involved? How will the work involved be divided fairly?

As Family Managers, we have to permit family members to deal with their feelings about what's happening. Realize that family members may initially focus on the additional work they'll have to do or what they have to give up. People can handle only so much change at a time and can easily become overwhelmed and immobilized, so take things slowly.

Delegation

According to a Harvard University study, men who grew up during the Great Depression doing regular chores around the house were healthier, happier, and more successful in their adulthood jobs and families than those who didn't. Researchers believe early successes at chores inspired

the men to tackle more and more challenging tasks, building their levels of confidence and responsibility.

> A good manager: someone who has successfully trained others to discharge his or her responsibilities.

To my mind, working together as a
team with your spouse and children
offers several side benefits, not the least of which is getting to know
your kids better. And when the going gets rough, as it always will,
we'd all do well to remember that by teaching our kids to do chores
we're helping mold them into people who will grow up to be more self-
sufficient and caring individuals who know the value of teamwork. Look
at it this way: we're doing their future wives, husbands, bosses, and
coworkers a big favor by letting them participate in their own care and
feeding.

Each of us has a limited amount of time, talent, and resources. When
you delegate, you're saying, "All this needs to be done, but I can't do it
all." By delegating you save time and energy for the things that only you
can do. Take an inventory of all the things you do:

Mark the things that absolutely must be done.
Mark the things that need to be done.
Indicate who else could do these things, if anyone.
Consider delegating or dropping the activities someone else can do.

Activity   Who Else Could Do It?

_____
_____
_____
_____

As you and your team articulate your expectations and really communicate with each other, delegation becomes almost automatic. But first
you may need to sell the idea of teamwork.

Selling Your Family on Teamwork

FIVE TRUTHS ABOUT MARITAL TEAMWORK

Before you can expect your family to work as a team, you and your husband need to model what working together well looks like. This may be easier for some couples than for others. If you need some guidance, check out these facts:

1. *Men and women look at the same situation and tend to see different things.* Often men focus on one object and miss everything around it—things that are very apparent to women. The reason your husband may not be helpful may not be because he doesn't care, but because he simply doesn't see what needs to be done. When broaching the idea of teamwork, say that you don't intend to call all the shots, decide what needs to be done, or become Inspector White Gloves, following him around as he cleans.

2. *Guilt is a poor motivator.* It accomplishes little and many times worsens the situation. Instead of making your husband feel guilty for what he doesn't do, let him know how much you appreciate the help he already gives you. Then tell him you would like the whole family to work as a team. Appeal to his sense of fairness. Use language he understands—a sports analogy or an illustration from his work. In truth, men tend to understand the concept of teamwork quite well.

3. *Reason, not emotion, catches a man's attention.* Don't approach him when you feel resentful and overworked. Make a list of all the household tasks, then on a relaxed evening when no one is under stress, sit down and go over the list. Explain your dilemma, and ask his advice on getting the whole family in on the "fun." State your rationale clearly: it's good for the kids to have a responsibility to help, and bad for them not to. Things will run more smoothly, and you will have more energy for other activities. Listen as well as talk.

Maybe you or your spouse is starting a new career, moving your office to your home, working a different shift. Maybe you've added a new family member—an aging parent, a new baby, a foster child. Maybe family members are getting increasingly busy, starting to live in their own separate worlds, and you feel the need for pulling yourselves together as a family. All of these situations and many others require a change in the way you do things. You'll need to strategize. Whatever need, developing a team mentality is important. Enlist your husband's support in making the transition smooth.

4. *Asking gets you a lot further than telling.* After I was interviewed on TV concerning Family Management and team building, the producer of the show I appeared on, who is also a husband and father of three, told me his wife's secret to success. "She gives me choices," he said. "Men don't like to be told what to do—especially if it involves things they don't like to do or things about which they feel inept. My wife will hand me a list on Saturday of maybe twenty chores that need to be done around the house, and she'll ask me to pick ten or twelve. This way I can choose what I feel I can succeed at."

5. *He needs to know you're on his team before he joins yours.* Men and women who demand that the other person meet their needs first always end up short. Go ahead, ask for help in lightening your load, but make sure you are doing your part to ease the stresses in his life. Your appeal will have immeasurably more weight.

ACCENTUATE THE POSITIVE

Remember you're selling the idea of teamwork, first to your spouse, then to your children. Whenever we buy something, we want to know what we'll get from the product or service. "What will it do for me?" is an entirely reasonable question for a family team member to ask.

Be realistic. Nobody likes buying something from a salesperson who makes wild claims about his or her product. Sometimes a benefit of buying into delegation is indirect: if everybody does chores, Mom will be less stressed, so there will be less conflict. Sometimes a benefit is

"Most people want to be part of a team." —Candice Kaspers

long term, sort of like taking vitamins every day. Children may not immediately see the benefit to them of learning to cook (although once they've started, they're likely to feel the satisfaction of having learned a new skill). But, believe me, when they're living on their own, as our son John is, they'll look back and see the long-term benefits. And sometimes, of course, a benefit is readily apparent. They'll see immediately that you can take them to the science museum Saturday afternoon if they help you clean the house Saturday morning. And because their rooms are clean, they'll be able to find their shoes!

Conduct a Family Manager Workshop for Your Team

Businesses use seminars and workshops for any number of reasons: to teach people new skills, to work intensively to plan new project launches, and to give people who will be working closely together a chance to get to know each other's strengths and weaknesses and to form a coherent team. Your family team members probably know each other pretty well. But if you're trying to introduce the idea of teamwork to your family or if you're contemplating a major project—anything from moving to a new city to making some fairly drastic changes in your everyday routines—taking a weekend to have a "management" seminar might be one of the best things you ever did.

1. *Planning.* List for yourself and your family what will be covered at your "seminar." Get input; from the start, show that the family will operate as a democracy and that each member counts. Create anticipation by promising surprises, appetizing snack breaks, and free time and prizes as rewards for participation. You might pick a weekend when you can get away to someplace with a retreat atmosphere. You might rent a cabin or camp out at a state park.

Make sure you have all the supplies you'll need—poster board and markers for brainstorming, a notebook for the recording secretary, the proper clothing and sports equipment for everyone, books for quiet times, games, and so on. In the spirit of teamwork, you might give each family member a list of things he/she is responsible for gathering by the morning the seminar starts.

Plan to cover only one or two areas in the first meeting. The eventual goal will be to look at what can be done by the team in each of the seven Family Management departments. But seven categories is a lot for any group to cover. So take it slow. There's always another day.

2. *Execution.* Wherever you gather, make sure the phone is turned off (mobile phones included). While you are there, play some old favorite games or some new ones and then talk about the way you play together—a great team-building exercise. Who's most competitive? Who likes to play with a partner or on a team? Who enjoys going it alone?

Another way to begin is to create a master wish list that you can come back to again and again, even if each person's wish isn't on this meeting's agenda. Again, let everyone participate. An overall list might look something like this:

I want laundry folded and put away when it comes out of the dryer—
not heaped in a pile on the sofa for two days.

I want the kitchen to be cleaned once a day.

I'd like to know that when I bring my friends home after the game on
Friday night, there's a pretty good chance we'll have some snacks
around.

I'd like to walk into the family room and not see filthy socks on the
floor.

I'd like the dogs to smell better.

I'd like the bathrooms to be cleaned once a week.

I want a place where I can keep my model projects out to work on.

I don't want to cook every night.

How much each person can participate in your family chore system will vary with your family members' ages, abilities, and interests. Talk about jobs that need to be done and who the best candidates are to do them.

For the "formal" parts of your seminar, have a recording secretary. If you have a specific topic, like deciding how the laundry gets done or the house gets cleaned on a regular basis, brainstorm ideas and have the secretary take notes.

Devise a master chore list of some sort. At home you will post it in a place where everyone can see it. Make chore assignments specific and realistic. "Just do your best" or "Help around the house more" are too general. Spell out the tasks for kids in as much detail as possible, such as "Use a large plastic bag to collect trash from all household trash cans every Monday and Thursday. Tie the bag and put it in the outside garbage can before you leave for school." (Be realistic about the age-appropriateness of tasks. Five-year-olds can unload dishwashers, but not if the dishes go on high shelves.)

Another idea is to have everyone think about what it means to be a team or to give a minitalk on that subject, emphasizing that a team is a group of people who work together for the common good of all of them. You may also schedule small-group working sessions. Perhaps you and your husband can take some time to work on a budget while your children use newsprint or poster board to make a new chores schedule, reflecting the decisions you've made. Or you might want to delegate to your children the task of coming up with a system of rotation that gets the kitchen and the bathrooms cleaned regularly.

Make sure you plan time for frequent breaks, especially if you have younger children. In addition to scheduled team recreation and game playing, schedule quiet or alone time.

3. *Follow up.* For the first few weeks after the seminar, set up a regular weekly time, perhaps at dinner on a weeknight or on a Sunday afternoon, to solicit feedback on how the new routines are working. Use this time to make changes as necessary and to reemphasize that you're a team doing a new thing together or doing the same things in a different way. Make it clear that honest mistakes are allowable, that new methods take time to become second nature.

The benefits from a Family Management seminar are many:

• You get everything out in the open, on the table. Family members have a chance to share both their frustrations and things they think are working well. In the case of a Family Management seminar to establish new cleaning routines, everybody buys into the program. Ideally no one feels he has had something thrust on him he didn't agree to. This also creates less stress for the Family Manager because she doesn't have to think up all the answers or be an enforcer.

• You can make fun the reward for a job well done. When you get together to brainstorm during a seminar, think of ways to save money as well as time. For instance, if you were using a cleaning service before, what will you do with the money you save? Or if you have to stop using the cleaning service because of a tight budget, what "compensation" can you offer your new cleaning service, your family? Can you, for example, go out to lunch and a few rounds of miniature golf or bowling on Saturday afternoon after a run-through of the house in the morning?

• Even the youngest kids feel like they have input and more control over their lives. Happy employees are those who feel empowered by bosses who listen to their concerns and have work environments in which workers participate in figuring out how to do their jobs, rather than being told exactly when, where, and how they are to perform. Such employees feel they have control over their lives and "own" part of the results of their work. Why should kids be any different?

> "It is useless to make a formal decision with which group members informally disagree." —William G. Dyer

Ten Tips for Making Your Team Successful

Whatever you undertake together as a team, these ten tips can help put you all on the winning side.

1. Update chore lists periodically. Each family team member should have the opportunity to raise the issue of switching jobs as his or her skill level and schedule demands change.
2. Remember that challenging assignments are good. Be sure to cheer your team members on in their pursuits.
3. Expect imperfect work, but shower your child with praise for effort. "You did an excellent job of washing the dishes, but please try to remember to clean out the sink after you've finished."
4. Offer age-appropriate rewards for the completion of certain tasks. A cookie, an extra hour of television, or an evening with the car builds morale as well as strengthening the chore system.

An Aside on Rewards

There are many schools of thoughts about kinds of reward for work. I tend to stay away from monetary rewards for everyday chores. But when our boys do an above-and-beyond-the-normal-call-of-duty job—put insulation in the attic to cut down our utility bill, paint a room, scrub mildew off the ceiling of a big porch—we pay them. Another exception is our near-annual garage sale, in which the whole family participates and takes a share of the profits to use as they see fit. I tend to think that kids are better motivated in the long run by the realization that if everybody works together, their home is a happier place to be. When the boys were younger, I would reward extra chores with chits or gold stars, which could be traded in for things like lunch out with Dad or Mom or a special outing. Also schedule fun errands after a day of hard work, so that washing and vacuuming the cars without complaining might be followed up by a trip to get a bike repaired and new tires put on. Reward yourselves as a whole team when you finish a big job. Did you spend half the day spring-cleaning the yard? Celebrate by going out to dinner.

5. Be a positive role model. To get enthusiasm, you have to give it.

6. Look for ways to make jobs fun. Set the kitchen timer and have contests to see how much you can get done in twenty minutes. Play bouncy music and dance with your broom and mop. Make a simple cape for a young child to become the superhero Laundryman to wear when folding laundry.

7. Express confidence in your family's ability to do a good job. A Family Manager's positive expectations create an atmosphere for better performance.

8. Encourage family members to be creative in developing their own ways to accomplish jobs. This is another way of being supportive and positive. When someone has a new idea, your first response should be "Try it," not "That won't work." That is, within reason—a creative way for a kid to clean his bedroom is probably *not* to shovel everything under the bed. But it might be that you've got a visually motivated child who likes to be able to see where things are kept. If she likes to organize things in the basement, where things are on open shelves, you might consider installing open shelves in her room. Be willing to spend time brainstorming with team members.

9. Continually look for ways to mesh family members' skills or hobbies and the chores. Some ideas: The teenager who is desperate to drive the family car could drive it more if he or she ran errands. A child who likes to arrange things in categories could volunteer to reorganize the games and sports equipment or the pantry.

10. On a regular basis, make time for fun, team-building excursions. When our kids were younger, we'd often get up early on Saturday morning, drive to a nearby state park, and cook breakfast on an open fire. After puttering around the woods and skipping rocks on the lake for a couple of hours, we would go home and tackle our Saturday chores.

The Triangle at Work

> "Work and play are an artificial pair of opposites because the best kind of play contains an element of work, and the most productive kind of work must include something of the spirit of play."   —Sydney J. Harris

I've said it before, but I'll say it again: Don't try to make too many changes at once. Building a team takes time. You might begin with one or two areas of your home or kinds of chores, like food preparation or laundry, and branch out from there. You and your husband should also agree to be honest and loving about disagreements you may have about your expectations. For instance, his mother may have kept a hospital-clean home, so he thinks the kitchen should be cleaned three times a day, while once daily suits you fine. You need to talk this out and negotiate a compromise you both can live with.

I know that whenever I've decided to expand our task force into new areas, increase others' responsibilities for things that used to be "mom's job," I've had better success if I talked my proposals over with Bill before taking them to the whole family. Let me also add here that you might be pleasantly surprised when you bring up the idea of sharing chores. My kids thought about hiring a marching band to celebrate when their father took over more of the cooking. I know one woman whose daughter decided when she was about ten that she'd really like to have her socks matched up in her drawer, so she volunteered to start doing her own laundry.

Messy Can Be Good

If one of your team wants a place she can keep messy while she works on building models or sewing or science experiments, try to work with her so that a corner of her room or the basement or the garage can be hers for just that purpose. (I'm a firm believer in the principle that messiness engenders creativity.)

Using communication and delegation to reach mutually agreed-upon expectations is work. Some days it's going to seem like more work than doing it all yourself. On those days, remind yourself that Family Management and team building are about developing the best in you and your family, not just about cleaning the house or doing the laundry. Knowing how to operate as a member of a team is a skill that will prove invaluable in your child's life.

On other days, you're probably going to feel like you're not getting anywhere. Think about triangulation and navigation again for a moment. If a ship's captain kept sailing toward the *same* third point over and over, nobody would ever have made it to these shores. Where you are keeps changing and so does where you want to go. Communication, delegation, and expectations are not fixed points. They're part of an ongoing process.

When expectations aren't met, communicate with each other about changing your delegating system or your expectations. When communication gets heated, remind yourselves what your expectations are and that one of them is to work together in a mutually worked-out delegation. When delegated duties go undone, communicate, communicate, communicate after you reexamine your expectations.

But on many, even most, days you'll reap the rewards of team building in a cleaner, cozier, calmer home. You won't be feeling frazzled because you're trying to do it all yourself. You won't be feeling martyred. You can, and should, pat yourself and your team members on the back for making your family a place where everybody works together.

Keeping Your Balance

- Communication + Delegation → Expectations.
- Self-imposed martyrdom doesn't help anyone.
- An unspoken expectation is an impossible expectation.
- Teamwork means everyone gets a say.
- Make sure every team member knows what's in it for him or her.
- Assure your family—in word and deed—that you're on their team before you expect them to join yours.
- Reevaluate and renegotiate as needed (which will be often).
- Make fun the reward for a job well done.
- A good manager is someone who has successfully trained others to discharge his or her responsibilities.
- Bear in mind that when your kids grow up they won't remember if the kitchen floor was mopped every day, but they will remember if home was a fun place to be.

SIX
Work Smarter, Not Harder

"Order is the shape upon which beauty depends." —Pearl S. Buck

I like to think of myself as creative, competent, and flexible. Ergo, I used to think *routine* was a dirty word. Who'd want to clean the bathroom every Tuesday? Become tied down to a regular time to shop for groceries? Pay the bills on the same day of the month? I liked to keep the creditors guessing.

Routines didn't come about overnight in our family. Only repeated frustration led to a cure. It was mornings that pushed me over the edge, and they usually ran something like this: Our music alarm would go off first. I usually slept through it, but the music woke Bill enough to realize he was freezing because I'd stolen all the covers again. I would pretend not to hear him complain. Then the second alarm—the one on Bill's wristwatch—would go off. Music and beeping, and still we were in bed. Five minutes later, the third alarm would buzz. Bill put this clock on the bookshelf, far enough away so he had to stretch to turn the alarm off, but not so far he had to get out of bed. A few minutes later, the fourth would sound in the bathroom, which meant I had to get out of bed to turn it off.

I'd throw on a robe and manage to clear a path down the hall. Every morning was an adventure. Would I trip over the dog? The schoolbooks? The laundry basket? Would I live to see the kitchen?

"Habit is either the best of servants or the worst of masters." —Nathaniel Emmons

I'd reach the kitchen only to discover we were out of milk again. Now where did I put that grocery list? About that time, the dog would bark to be let out. Shortly thereafter, the boys would begin their morning litany. They wanted to know where their clean shirts, their socks, their school projects, and their library books were. You name it, they'd lost it, and they needed it now. No wonder I often felt tempted to go back to bed. I silently vowed to ground the first kid who said, "Why can't we have pancakes every morning? Other kids do."

One day something snapped (my last nerve ending). I was probably caffeine deprived, since we ran out of coffee at least as often as we ran out of milk. When I calmed down a bit I realized that school and work were stressful enough without the added aggravation of starting our days hurried and cranky. Things had to change.

Routine Relief

Do you find yourself expending the same energy on the same conflicts? Getting the kids off to school? Or trying to listen attentively to your family's accounts of their day while stirring dinner, feeding the cat, transferring clothes from washer to dryer, and setting the table? Or making sure the bills are paid and mailed before the due date? There's no magic wand you can wave over every day's to-do list that will make days and nights run smoothly.

There is an alternative: routines. Systems, routines, and standard operating procedures are essential to every business. Everyone needs to know who is responsible for what, what the freedoms and restrictions are, and how to follow an assignment through. Successful families need the benefits of routines as well. Our family is living proof that wild mornings—and afternoons and evenings—can be tamed.

The hundreds of tasks, large and small, required to keep a family running can usually be fitted into routines that keep you from having to reinvent the wheel every time a library book is missing or the garbage needs to go out. Once you decide how, when, and by whom something should be done, you eliminate questions and arguing. Time and energy are no longer wasted on the trivial.

Routines enable us to spend time and energy on the important things, like going to the park with our son to fly a kite, helping our daughter think through a problem, curling up under a quilt to read, or talking as a family about what we'd like to do together this weekend, and then having the time to do it. Routines help us eradicate time-stealers and replace them with the wonderful commodity of time itself. They also make it easier to stick to our priorities. Deciding what needs to be accomplished and then establishing a routine to do it frees us to do what is truly important to us. And routines give our children a sense of security because they know what to expect.

Many Family Managers have told me that once their children get accustomed to new routines, they religiously adhere to them because of the order and harmony these routines promote. In fact, many family routines end up becoming cherished family traditions—playing a board game after homework is finished at night, going out for breakfast with Daddy on Saturday mornings, playing Sock Wars when the laundry's finished. (This is a favorite at our house. After the socks are matched and rolled into balls, we clear the family room of breakables, play the theme from *Star Wars*, and throw socks at each other.)

Our new morning routine began with me, a pad of paper, a pen, and a cup of coffee. I listed every stress point about mornings I could think of and possible solutions: start earlier, maintain consistent bedtimes on school nights, collect things they'd need for school the next morning the night before, have a shelf by the door for each member of the family, and place a kitty in the kitchen for last-minute needs for

> Routines give our children a sense of security because they know what to expect.

> "To learn new habits is everything, for it is to reach the substance of life."
> —Henri Frédéric Amiel

incidental cash. (I didn't really solve the milk and coffee part of the problem, though, until a few years later when I started going to the grocery store early in the morning.) We had a family meeting talk about it, and the boys had some ideas, too. We tried the new routine. To my amazement, our home started to run more smoothly. Even more exciting, my family liked the new system. It seems they prefer not having to rush around in the morning.

In the years since that meeting, we've made great progress. When we saw how much relief a morning routine brought, we designed others for each of the seven Family Management areas.

Is the process simple? No. Routines take time to become, well, routine. You have to plan for adjustment and readjustment periods as you discover what works and what doesn't. But this I'm confident of: routines can help drive the frenzy out of your family.

When you set out to impose routines, remember that every routine has ramifications. We've all been frustrated by so-called customer service clerks who won't—or to be fair, aren't allowed to—return our $1.39 for the defective part we bought unless we fill out a form in triplicate, copy it, send it by registered mail to the address they give us, and wait until the third full moon of the next month that ends in r. What do we do? Write off the money, chalk it up to experience, and vow never to do business with that company again.

Maybe you're the kind of person who bristles at the thought of routines. If you think routines are rigid, maybe even a little boring, think about what it would be like to do business in a world without routines. If there's no set time to do certain things, there's a good chance those things won't get done. Our kids miss practices and birthday parties because we didn't know when these were. We get frustrated and cranky because we're constantly playing catch-up and wasting precious time and energy trying to figure out what to do next or where we put something. Take it from a woman after your own heart. I love to be flexible and spontaneous. But the truth is, because routines add order

> "Well begun is half done."
> —Aristotle

and sanity to life, they allow us to be *more* flexible and spontaneous.

Before You Begin

Whether you call them that or not, it's likely you already have some standard operating procedures. The trick is identifying the routines that work and taking them a step further to make them work harder for you and your family. Maybe it's your practice to wash the bedsheets once a week. To turn this practice into a time-saving routine, set a specific day of the week for your family to take their sheets off their beds and put them in the laundry room before they leave the house. Then after school, one of the kids' chores can be to put the clean sheets back on the beds. As you consider the routines you have and the ones you want to initiate, remember:

1. *Start small. Rome and IBM weren't built in a day.* Maybe you're ready to identify every instance when your children bicker about whose turn it is to do what, and plan to write an exhaustive sibling procedure guidebook that covers every possible interaction between your children 365 days a year. When you're thinking about routines, don't try to make one for every possible situation. You'll drive yourself nuts.

Instead, start with one particularly regular and frustrating situation. When our boys were little they couldn't get in the car without rancorous dispute about whose turn it was to sit in the front seat. We got tired of this daily duel, so we instituted a routine: each boy would have a turn sitting in the front seat for one month. The boys knew on the first day of each month that it was another brother's turn, and they kept track of this themselves. Of course, when they got their driver's licenses, this was no longer an issue. So that routine fell by the wayside.

Traffic control engineers identify certain city intersections where accidents occur and then put up traffic lights or warning signs to reduce the risk of collision. When we institute routines, we do well to look for problem intersections—where chores that need to be done frequently collide with stress or bickering. Routines are like those traffic lights and warning signs. They don't entirely eliminate problems, but they reduce the number of problems. If specific issues arise only occasionally, you probably don't need a routine.

2. *Rethink the old adage "If it ain't broke, don't fix it."* Recently I heard a business consultant scoff at that concept. To stay on the cutting edge, the new adage is: If it's working, look at *how* it's working to meet today's needs and see if you can make it better.

Let's use a simple example. Say you have the routine of cooking burgers on the grill every Friday night. You've been doing it so long you don't ever think about what you're going to have for dinner on Friday nights. It's a ritual your family enjoys. So why not instigate some other no-brainer meals, like every Tuesday you cook chicken?

Or sometimes things that have been working for a long time and still seem to be working can use some fine-tuning. Suppose you've always cleaned the house by working together on Saturday mornings. You all work well together and generally everything is done by noon. Basically this is not a "broken" system. But if someone on your team suggested that you could get just as much done if you all cleaned for half an hour every evening, leaving you Saturday mornings free to play, you might well change the routine.

3. *If it is broken, fix it.* This is the place from which I started my morning routines. Identify the stress-producing situations that occur on a regular basis. Just like you'd tackle a problem at work—say, missed deadlines or product packaging that keeps tearing—gather your team and brainstorm about ways to solve the problem.

The general rule of thumb in business when you're looking to fix problems is to look to the most crucial first. In a family those could be the most annoying, like our morning chaos. If your family members are regularly missing doctor's appointments, scheduled practices, group meetings, and even social engagements, maybe it's time to establish a master calendar. If your electric bill is soaring and you notice that lights are left on every time you leave the house, you might appoint a light monitor whose job is to routinely walk through the house and make sure all lights are out before you leave. (To get the family working on this problem as a team, empower the light monitor to fine anyone who leaves bedroom or bathroom lights on—including Mom and Dad.) Or you might have more costly problems. If you have no routine for paying bills on time, you might convince yourself that you need one simply by looking at the amount of penalties and interest you pay on overdue bills over the course of a year.

4. *Businesses and families are organic entities.* That is to say, in families, as in businesses, all systems are interrelated. As you institute new routines, make sure you're not causing a problem somewhere else. If your new routine is for your twelve-year-old to vacuum the house before he leaves for school on Thursdays, make sure this is not a morning when your husband sleeps in because he worked the night shift. That one seems obvious. But sometimes it's the obvious that escapes our notice. Be aware that you'll likely want to fine-tune routines over time. Maybe in a flush of enthusiasm your eighth-grader volunteered for more chores than she could actually do. (Well, it's been known to happen.) Or maybe the new routine is working just fine until your teenager starts Advanced Placement English and has three hours of homework every night. Periodically reviewing and adjusting routines is good for everyone.

5. *Consult the experts and adapt, adapt, adapt.* My longtime friend Peggy is superorganized. When we lived across the hall from each other in college, I noticed that her closet, drawers, and desk were always in order, her laundry always done before she ran out of clean underwear,

> "Nothing is more powerful than a habit."   —Ovid

and her checkbook always balanced. There were days I didn't know whether to salute her or stick my tongue out at her. What was her secret? Was I missing a gene? Was it because I was bottle-fed instead of breast-fed? Was it the way I was potty-trained?

I remember when, early in my career as a Family Manager, I realized the green gunk was taking over our shower and the dust bunnies were multiplying under every piece of furniture at an alarming rate. When I got brave enough to seek help, I called Peggy and asked her to share her secrets. Her success, fortunately, was catching, and her systems rescued our household. Never be afraid to ask for help. When it's within reach, take it! (Note: Peggy visited my house a week ago and commented, "Kathy, I can't believe how smoothly your house runs and how organized you've become. Why, you used to be the messiest, most disorganized person I knew." Yes, there is hope for anyone!)

There's No Time Like the Present

Routines only become routines if we create them. Take a few minutes right now to think about the consistent stress points in your family. If you're having trouble identifying them, maybe this list will help. You could use it in a few different ways. Review the events of the last week or so in your mind. Put a slash mark for every time a problem came up in that area. The area with the most slash marks is probably where you should start.

Or jot down a description of the problems you see in each area. Read the problems over again. Start with the area that makes your blood boil.

You might also consider getting input from your husband and other family members. When I finally brought up changing our laundry routine, I couldn't have been more pleased at the response I got. Everybody was frustrated and everybody had ideas about what would work.

Inventing the New Routine and Putting It to Work for You

Pick *one* or *two* problem areas to tackle with new routines. The more areas you try to modify at once, the fewer your chances of success.

> "Before we can move into a new arrangement, we must first go through a period of de-rangement."
> —M. C. Richards

Jot down ideas you have that might work as part of a new routine. Talk with your spouse. Get his input. Then call a family meeting, or talk with family members who will be affected by the routine. Remember that talking doesn't mean dictating terms, and in families, as in businesses, people are more apt to buy into new ways of doing things if they have some input into what those new ways are.

You might begin by stating the problem, saying something like, "I've been thinking we haven't been sitting down to eat dinner together as a family very much anymore. I'd like to know how you feel about that." Blaming and resentment shouldn't be part of the problem statement. If

Routines Can Help with . . .

Meal planning
Food shopping
Cooking and preparing meals
Cleaning up after meals
Straightening up the house
Vacuuming
Making beds
Doing laundry
Cleaning bathrooms
Collecting and putting out trash
Recycling

Assisting with/doing homework
Shopping for clothing
Family paperwork—finances and bill
  paying
Errands
Clothes to dry cleaners
Car maintenance
Yard work
Watering plants
Caring for pets

you are upset with your spouse or a child about some issue, the family meeting about solving a problem with a routine is not the place to discuss it.

If your family members give you blank looks or say that things are fine with them, tell them why things aren't fine with you. If you're discussing family dinners, you might tell them you're concerned about falling out of touch with each other and about not eating healthy food at a decent hour. You might also mention why this is a problem now when it wasn't before—for example, you've been working longer hours and not had as much time to fix dinner lately. Maybe you really don't like to cook all that much and are fresh out of ideas for good, nutritional meals and simply want some help with the cooking and shopping.

Solicit everybody's opinions about the need for a new routine. Then ask for suggestions about what would work. At this stage, all ideas, no matter how far out, are fodder for the discussion. Don't dismiss anyone's ideas out of hand. Simply list them all on a piece of paper. Then you can group them into categories and discuss the relative merits of everything from eating out every night (probably not a reasonable option) to sharing cooking chores on a regular rotating basis—maybe week by week or night by night. If it's week by week, the person who's cooking the next week could, with your help if necessary, plan menus the week before. The shopper, whether it's you or someone else, would then have a weekly list. The chef moves from chef one week to cleanup crew the next.

There are about as many ways to organize this as there are families. Perhaps you'll decide to have biweekly family cook-ins, where you all work together to put food in the freezer for the next two weeks. Whatever you decide to do, be as realistic and as simple as possible. Don't make overly elaborate arrangements you know you're not capable of following through on. Be sure that children are assigned or volunteer for age-appropriate tasks in the system.

Pick a day to start your new routine. Mark the occasion with some kind of celebration, even if it's only a small ritual of hanging the schedule on the refrigerator door or offering a toast to the new chef during his or her first dinner. After a week or so, and again in a month or so, evaluate the routine.

> "You may have to fight a battle more than once to win it."
> —Margaret Thatcher

Give everyone a chance to speak his or her piece. What do they like about it? What do they hate? What would they like to change? Make adjustments as needed. Remember the routine is there to help you; you and your family aren't there to serve the routine.

Even a seemingly sensible routine like a before-bed cleanup is sometimes hard to enforce. You don't want to get into useless power struggles. If your child is feeling overly tired that night and needs to be in bed, do you keep her up until the room is cleaned up? Do you then fight to get her up in the morning?

Winning Advice

As I've said before, I am a great believer in consulting the experts and sharing information. Even the experts themselves recognize the need to learn from each other. That's why CEOs in industries as different as publishing and electronics meet periodically to share ideas, even if they are in some cases in direct competition. What's good for one company can be good for a whole industry. And you can always put your own spin on it. What follows is shared information, from Family Managers I've talked to and worked with and from my own experience. Feel free to try any of the ideas here. Adapt them to fit your needs. For more ideas, network with your family and friends. Pass your good ideas along. What's good for one family can be good for a whole country full of families.

This list includes everything from itty-bitty routines to larger standard operating procedures. Sometimes the smallest changes, ones that can be incorporated overnight, make a difference all

> A big part of the battle to be a good Family Manager is choosing the right battles.

Two-timing Routines

No two of us are alike. But we all have at least two things in common. First, none of us will ever have more than twenty-four hours in a day (and it's a pretty sure bet there will never be less to do in those twenty-four hours). And second, we'd all like to accomplish more in less time. This being the case, I am constantly looking for ways to do two things at once. Doubling up on tasks has become routine for my family and me. This way, we have more time for family fun.

To get your crew in the swing of two-timing routines, start by identifying tasks or projects that don't require your full attention. Then make a list of things you can do at the same time. Post the list in a central location. Every time you "catch" someone doubling up, offer words of praise, or give a weekly reward to the person who does it best.

- Get family members in the habit of never walking through the house empty-handed. Pick up as you go.
- Kids can fold clothes and watch cartoons. Have them put P.E. clothes directly into their gym bags.
- Ask teenagers to throw in a load of laundry before starting their homework. When they take a snack break, it will be time to put the wash in the dryer.
- Show kids how to strip beds and take dirty linens to the washer while you change the sheets.
- Teach preschoolers to identify colors while cleaning up. Pick up all the blue toys first, then red, black, yellow, etc.
- Have young kids wash patio furniture and bicycles while the older ones wash the car and the dog.
- The whole family can divide and conquer a trip to the mall or discount store with separate lists.
- Wash the medicine cabinet's mirror and shine sink fixtures while watching your child take a bath.
- The next time the kids have a bubble bath, have them swish their hands and feet around the water line to loosen up a bathtub ring.
- As long as you're in the kitchen making dinner, check on staples and make a grocery list.
- Talk on the phone while putting away groceries.
- Wash dishes or unload the dishwasher while waiting for the water to boil.

- Cook two, three, or four meals at once. Clean carrots for tonight's pot roast, afternoon snacks, and tomorrow night's salad.
- Make soup and stew at the same time. Double the recipes of both and you'll have tonight's dinner plus three more for the freezer.
- Before you run errands, think about what else might need to be dropped off or picked up nearby.
- Stock up for the future. If you're buying deodorant or mascara, consider buying two or three so you won't have to make that trip again.
- While you're watching a family television show, have everyone jump up during the commercials, pick up clutter, and put it away.
- While working out on an exercise bike or step machine, look through mail-order catalogs to get gift ideas and plan purchases.
- Give the dog a bath while you water the garden.
- Steam away wrinkles in a garment by hanging it in the bathroom while you shower.

out of proportion with their size. That's because small changes are easier for people in businesses and families to get used to. Some of the larger routines will no doubt take longer to implement. Remember to go back and evaluate and fine-tune after the routine has been in place for a while.

Routine Ideas

TIME AND SCHEDULING

Set up a home base of operation, a place from which you organize and administer the countless daily details you oversee: schedules, appointments, invitations, phone numbers, school papers. I call my base of operation Control Central. Place a file for each child in this home base, choosing a different color for each child. When the kids come home from school, have them stop at Control Central and place important papers, forms, and other school information in their files. Make a master schedule of family activities and post it in a central place. Keep a pen near it and make each person who's old enough responsible for adding his or her new items. Have bright-colored sticky notes to signal an important detail or an addition that requires transportation.

Create a morning chore chart. Post it at kids' eye level on the refrigerator or on a kitchen bulletin board. Part of your morning routine is for the kids to look at it and do whatever chores they need to before school.

Designate a roomy drawer or a large basket in the kitchen for errands: shoes to be repaired, film to be dropped off, books to be returned to the library.

Post an exit routine by your door as a visual reminder of what needs to be done. Here's the way one family does it:

Exit Routine

Kids
- ❏ Lunch box/meal card
- ❏ Backpack/books/papers
- ❏ House key
- ❏ Gym clothes
- ❏ Rain gear/outerwear
- ❏ Emergency money
- ❏ Musical instrument
- ❏ Other _____

Mom and Dad
- ❏ Dry cleaning
- ❏ Bank deposit
- ❏ Library books
- ❏ Letters/packages to mail
- ❏ Lights and appliances off
- ❏ Answering machine on
- ❏ Frozen food out to thaw
- ❏ Doors locked
- ❏ Briefcase
- ❏ Car keys
- ❏ Purse
- ❏ Security system activated

FOOD

Set up a dinner preparation routine. Alert your family ten minutes before dinner is ready so they can wash hands and do preassigned tasks: set the table, prepare beverages, help serve plates, or put food on the table.

Write a family menu of various meal choices. Every Sunday night, let each family member order the meal for one night that week. Post the resulting weekly menu on the refrigerator door. The first parent or teenager home knows what to start for dinner. (School administrative assistant Stacy Ross says this works well in her family of six. Her kids love the idea of ordering from a menu.)

Make a permanent grocery and drugstore shopping list—foods, dry goods, paper products, cleaning supplies, toiletries, etc. Make copies and fill in each week before you shop.

Create a grocery shopping routine. If you buy in bulk, shop once a month at a wholesale club. Then pick a time each week to go to the grocery store—preferably when crowds are sparse. Or hire a responsible teenager to shop for you once a week.

Create an efficient grocery-day routine.

Bag your own groceries so you can put things together the way they go in your kitchen.

Put up groceries and prepare food for the week at the same time:

- Wash and prepare salad greens and store in plastic containers in the refrigerator for the week.
- Brown as much ground meat as you'll need for the week.
- Chop all onions and green peppers you plan to use. Put in plastic sandwich bags and freeze.
- Hard-cook eggs.
- Cut up veggie sticks for snacks and lunches.
- Make individual-size packets of raisins, chips, cookies, etc., for lunch boxes.

Go to the farmers' market on Saturdays in the summer. Make it a family outing and enjoy fresh vegetables and fruit for dinner all week long.

Begin a tradition of picking berries every August or apples in the fall as a family. Make jam or applesauce.

Try an alternating cooking arrangement. Your husband cooks on Mondays and Wednesdays; you cook on Tuesdays and Thursdays; eat out on Fridays, and be flexible about Saturdays and Sundays.

FINANCES

Pick a particular day of the week—not Friday afternoon—to make deposits and pick up needed cash for the week.

Set a time close to when you receive your bank statement to balance your checkbook and reconcile your statement.

Try to adjust your bills so that you're writing checks once or twice a month only. You may need to see if you can renegotiate some of the billing dates on your credit cards, and your mortgage may be a few days late, but there's always a grace period. You might even create a bill-paying routine and turn this distasteful chore into a pleasant experience. I sit down twice a month, brew some interesting coffee, play a favorite movie soundtrack CD, put fragrance oil on a lightbulb ring, sit by a sunny window, and write checks with a favorite pen.

Have a once-a-year planning session with your spouse. Plan for big expenditures and be sure to include money for vacations and fun. If or when you hit a rocky spot, solicit ideas from everyone who's old enough to talk about how to spend less money. Get creative. A seven-year-old may volunteer to have a less expensive at-home birthday party. Teenagers may volunteer to buy their prom dress at a second-hand shop or rent one from a local theater company, or rent their tux rather than buy one.

One mom told me her secret of saving money for Christmas presents. She clips coupons each week and shops at a grocery store that has a branch bank on site. She started the routine of getting cash refunds for her coupons (instead of having the amount deducted from her bill) and immediately depositing that money in the bank each week before she left the store.

Depending on their ages, create a routine for your kids to earn and be responsible for their own spending money. At our house, in keeping with my bent to adapt business management concepts to the home, James writes me a proposal—sort of an informal contract—that states what daily tasks, household chores, and extra odd jobs he will be in charge of in exchange for a weekly "paycheck."

Make the decision to let everything you buy replace or displace something you already have.

FAMILY MEMBERS AND FRIENDS

Start routines to do something enjoyable regularly—even if it's brief—with each of your children. Get a frozen yogurt on the way home from dance practice, take a walk after dinner on minimal-homework nights, read one chapter aloud from a book each night.

Set up a homework routine for your kids. Decide how much TV they can watch and when they will do homework. Stick with your decision.

Savvy Shopping Routines

- Wear easy-to-slip-off garments when shopping for clothes.
- Shop whenever possible by mail-order catalog instead of driving from store to store.
- Make a personal source guide. When you discover a store that has products you like at good prices, make a note and write down the phone number.
- When purchasing something new, consider the maintenance involved. White rugs require a lot of cleaning. Linen garments take longer to iron.
- Buy clothing staples such as hosiery and underwear in bulk twice a year.
- Keep on hand presents for special occasions, wrapping paper and gift sacks, ribbon and enclosure cards.

Create a bedtime routine for young children. Make sure they go to the bathroom before going to bed. Put a glass of water by the bed of a child who frequently needs a drink. Have a night-light or flashlight handy if they tend to be frightened of the dark.

As your kids get older, weekend night routines become increasingly important. When our two oldest boys were in high school, they had a certain curfew and had to tell us where they would be. If something special was going on, they called to ask permission to stay out later. If they changed locations, they called to let us know.

Write an emergency information list for babysitters and make photocopies. Include phone numbers for fire, police, poison control, ambulance, your pediatrician, a local pharmacy, a neighbor who would help, and an in-town relative. Also list each child's name, birth date, and blood type. Leave a blank space to fill in the number where you'll be and the children's schedule—bath time, bedtime, homework routine, etc.

HOME AND PROPERTY

Create a master file system for all the important information you need to keep pertaining to your home: appliance-repair agreements, warranties, receipts—those things you need only when you need them. It's also helpful to have a home-maintenance log, a schedule of things that need to be done maybe only once a year (like changing the furnace filter), and a list of where important documents are located—birth certificates, immunization records, passports, financial statements. *The Essential Home Record Book* by Pamela K. Pfeffer (Plume, 1997) is an easy way to record and keep track of these details.

Have a nightly seven-minute pickup sprint. Set a timer for seven minutes. During that time everyone in the house picks up and puts away the accumulated clutter of the day. Toss out old newspapers, close cabinets and drawers, plump pillows and cushions, change cat litter, straighten pictures and lamp shades, put things where they belong. You'll be surprised how much you can get done.

Create work centers with all the supplies needed for the task—bill paying, baking, craft, package wrapping/mailing centers.

Start the routine of returning everything you get out back to where it belongs. (Ten minutes a day looking for misplaced items wastes sixty hours a year.)

Keep a lost-and-found basket in the front closet. Family members can stash things they find lying around the house. Everyone knows that this is the first place to look when he or she can't find something.

Every summer when you get home from your family vacation with lots of dirty clothes, start the routine of washing them at a Laundromat where you can do it all at once. Go through your piled-up mail while you're waiting.

Start a "first Saturday" routine for each season of the year. Make it a family occasion. On the first Saturday of spring (reschedule if need be because of weather) you rake the lawn, wash the windows, plant flowers. This is something that can happen every year. The details of whatever you really need done may change. On the first Saturday of summer you clean out the garage, have a garage sale, or haul extra things to a charitable organization. On the first Saturday of fall you change the furnace filter, clean the basement, store summer sports equipment and clothes.

Starting in January, clean out one closet every month until you're done.

SPECIAL PROJECTS

Start the routine of taking your calendar with you to the store in January to buy birthday and anniversary cards for the year. Get a few cards with get-well, sympathy, and congratulations messages to have on hand. Alternatively, buy special occasion boxes from Unicef around Christmas time.

Establish family birthday routines. Hang curling ribbon from your chandelier and have a special meal for the honoree. Go around the table and have each person say what he or she appreciates about the birthday person. Our boys know that no matter how old they get, they still have to wrestle with Dad to avoid a birthday spanking. (This routine is now hard on Bill, since John and Joel are now bigger than he is.)

Create "first things" celebrations. Celebrate a young child's first bicycle ride without training wheels, the first day of school, the first haircut, or the first tooth lost. Celebrate an older child's first day to drive a car.

Delegate holiday tasks and turn them into yearly routines: have a scavenger hunt every Valentine's Day (at our house we start with a clue on the bathroom mirror and the boys follow one clue to the next until they find their Valentine's present); organize a neighborhood bicycle parade and make homemade ice cream on the Fourth of July; go on a Labor Day picnic. One mom told me that as a result of her feeling overwhelmed trying to get Thanksgiving dinner cooked, they started the routine of Dad taking the kids on an overnight campout the night before Thanksgiving.

Have a garage sale every year after you spring-clean.

Write a vacation checklist. List items to pack and things to do before you leave. Make photocopies and use one copy for each trip to save planning and execution time.

PERSONAL MANAGEMENT

Every year give yourself a thorough evaluation of how you feel about yourself physically, intellectually, emotionally, socially, spiritually, and professionally. Let your answers help you create routines to help you grow in each area.

Schedule some regular time to exercise each week. Treat these times as you would any other appointment. If you can't find time to exercise at the gym, exercise to a workout video at home; wear tennis shoes when doing chores; bend, stretch, and move briskly; wear ankle or wrist weights when you're puttering around the house; do isometric arm exercises in the car when you're stuck in traffic.

Ask a dermatologist or cosmetologist to help you find a skin-care routine that works for you. Abide by it religiously.

Listen to inspiring books on cassette tapes when you're running errands. Take time out daily to read part of a book that lifts your spirits.

Decide to learn something new every year. In past years I've learned to tap-dance, conquered a new computer program, studied Shakespeare's writings. This year I want to learn to water-ski on one ski.

Create the routine of getting together on a regular basis with a few friends who encourage you. Maybe eat lunch together on the first Tuesday of every month.

Set aside some time each week to enjoy some solitude—quiet time reading a book; taking walks; soaking in a bubble bath; whatever you enjoy and whenever you can fit it in. Make sure everyone in the family understands that unless there is an emergency, this is your special time.

Routines You Shouldn't Skip
When under Stress

- Exercise, even if it's only twenty minutes of brisk walking.
- The five basic food groups. You want enduring energy. Sugar highs and alcohol lows are not what you need now.
- Bedtime stories or breakfast chats with your kids.
- Washing your hair. Looking bad will make you feel worse.
- A good night's sleep. Going without sleep will mess up your schedule for the next day.
- Your sense of humor. Everything is temporary.

Micro/Macro:
Finding the Balance That Works for You

The key to routines that work well and improve family harmony is finding a balance between too rigid and too loose. Generally speaking, each of us tends to micro- or macro-manage. The micro-manager sets up precise rules and routines about how things are done around the house. She is keen on the details; if something isn't done just so, someone pays. True, this woman's house rarely gets chaotic or out of control. The downside to being too far into micro regimes is that there's no room for flexibility. Forget a spur-of-the-moment Saturday matinee if the floor hasn't been mopped. Forget shopping for a new stereo when the local store has a sale because the purchase isn't budgeted until next month. Families with micro-managing moms are often stressed out trying to keep her happy.

I know a woman who insists that all toys and projects be put away before bedtime. Maybe that doesn't sound too harsh, but it wouldn't work at my house. You see, I'm more of a macro-manager: I study the big picture and decide what life skills I want my kids to leave home with. Creativity is higher on my list than neatness, so my routines take shape under that umbrella. My kids have always been allowed to have some kind of creative building or art project going all the time. Obviously they couldn't stop and put it away every night. I remember when the big boys were younger, they turned my living room into a GI Joe war zone. They tied string to the light fixtures and ran it down and tied it to furniture legs to make zip lines for their action figures; built forts with sofa pillows; established roadways and battle fronts. I had a rule that their mess could stay out for five days or until we needed the room for something else, whichever came sooner. Then they had to relocate.

The trick is to find the balance, enough chaos to breed creativity and enough order to enable things to run smoothly. I don't consider my method absolutely superior to my neat friend's. Tidiness is far from a

bad quality. I think ideally we should all
be somewhere in the middle—macro-
manager enough to see the big picture
and the long-term results of the routines

> "Chaos often breeds life, when order breeds habit."
> —Henry Adams

we create, and micro-manager enough to keep things sanitary and in
fairly decent order. Routines let us get the routine things out of the way.
They give us a tool for working smarter, not harder.

Keeping Your Balance

- Routines help us replace common time-stealers with the wonderful commodity of time itself.
- Assign routines to only consistent stress points.
- Routines take time to become routine.
- Because routines add order and sanity to life, they actually promote flexibility and spontaneity.
- Take existing procedures and sharpen them to work harder for your family.
- Find a balance between micro- and macro-managing techniques so that both creativity and order are honored.

SEVEN
Do More of What
You Do Best

"Do what you know best; if you're a runner, run, if you're a bell,
ring."
—Ignas Bernstein

It's important to understand something here, and understand it
down to your bones. You already are a competent, capable woman.
You clearly have innate talent, learned skills, and organizational
abilities, or you wouldn't have (1) both a family and career to tend, or
(2) time to read this book! As you go through these exercises of identifying and improving your skills, keep foremost in your mind that your
competence as a Family Manager is already established.

Of course, like everyone else, you have some areas you're not as
strong in. Welcome to the human race. I want to share a strategy with
you that has made a huge difference in my personal and professional
life: how to capitalize on your core competencies.

We're all good at something. Many times, though, we're more aware
of our weaknesses than of our strengths. Knowing our strengths and rec-
ognizing our successes can lead to finding, in the words of Jonathan
Swift, "a vein of gold which the owner knows not of."

Many people call what we're good at skills; others prefer to call
them by other names: God-given talents, gifts, aptitudes, or whatever.
The term you use doesn't matter so much as the understanding that
they are the essence of what you have to offer the world and what you

have to deal with in your jobs—both of them.

> "Success breeds confidence."
> —Beryl Markham

Right now, spend a few minutes thinking about what you are good at. What are you proud of? What work do you do that gives you a rush of pleasure? Focus on who you already are. If your thoughts center around what you'd like to be good at or what you think you should be good at or what you think other people think you should be good at, tell yourself gently and firmly that you are concentrating on what you are already good at.

To get your thinking process moving, use the following list to mark the skills and talents you possess. Write in more of your own.

I'M GOOD AT:

- ❏ Nurturing
- ❏ Encouraging
- ❏ Supporting
- ❏ Helping
- ❏ Mothering
- ❏ Delegating
- ❏ Leading
- ❏ Following directions
- ❏ Calculating
- ❏ Drawing
- ❏ Painting
- ❏ Nursing
- ❏ Inquiring
- ❏ Diagnosing
- ❏ Recruiting
- ❏ Interpreting
- ❏ Painting
- ❏ Knitting

- ❏ Singing
- ❏ Dancing
- ❏ Writing
- ❏ Analyzing
- ❏ Negotiating
- ❏ Handling money
- ❏ Working alone
- ❏ Working in groups
- ❏ Problem solving
- ❏ Marketing
- ❏ Meeting needs
- ❏ Picturing
- ❏ Imaging
- ❏ Planning
- ❏ Setting goals
- ❏ Forming strategies
- ❏ Meeting deadlines
- ❏ Directing
- ❏ Scheduling

- ❏ Fulfilling expectations
- ❏ Making a team
- ❏ Serving
- ❏ Editing
- ❏ Overcoming
- ❏ Pioneering
- ❏ Shaping
- ❏ Learning
- ❏ Fact finding
- ❏ Reading
- ❏ Overseeing
- ❏ Polishing
- ❏ Coordinating
- ❏ Facilitating
- ❏ Monitoring
- ❏ Influencing
- ❏ Enforcing
- ❏ Persuading

❑ Tutoring
❑ Advising
❑ Moving
❑ Preserving
❑ Sculpting
❑ Researching
❑ Evaluating
❑ Assessing worth
❑ Refinishing
❑ Decision making
❑ Visualizing
❑ Driving
❑ Conceptualizing
❑ Playing an
   instrument

❑ Collecting
❑ Developing
❑ Creating
❑ Weaving
❑ Assembling
❑ Organizing
❑ Structuring
❑ Gathering details
❑ Categorizing
❑ Producing
❑ Acting
❑ Presenting
❑ Identifying trends
❑ Crafting
❑ Speaking

❑ Communicating
❑ Teaching
❑ Solving problems
❑ Selling
❑ Cleaning
❑ Cooking
❑ Comforting people
❑ Coaching
❑ Singing
❑ Consulting
❑ Negotiating
❑ Resolving
❑ Lecturing
❑ Decorating
❑ Entertaining

Was this a tough assignment for you? The first time a friend of mine, a competent woman with a creative career, did it, she counted herself good at only two or three things. I asked her if she was serious, pointing out her career accomplishments, among other things. She said, "Well, yes, but . . ." As she did the exercise, she admitted she had been thinking only of her Family Manager career, and she really considered herself in the remedial class when it came to Family Management. Remember as you do this exercise that you're looking to identify your strengths—what you're good at doing—wherever you do them.

What we're good at is almost always what we enjoy doing. You need to identify the skills you have that you enjoy using most. These skills are transferable to almost any job you're doing regardless of where you first picked them up.

People rarely enjoy something they do very badly. Generally speaking, listing the skills you enjoy using most and listing the skills you do well are two different ways of arriving at the same list. If you had trouble with making a list of what you were good at, this might be a good time to make yourself a list of what you enjoy doing because the next thing I'm going to ask you to do is to think about how you can transfer what you're good at and enjoy doing to areas where you have real weaknesses. (And remember that every one of us has them!)

We need to know our strengths as much as we need to know our weaknesses. Emily Dickinson had a way with

> "Not to discover weakness is the artifice of strength."
> —Emily Dickinson
>
> "No one can produce great things who is not thoroughly sincere in dealing with himself."
> —James Russell Lowell
>
> "Too many people overvalue what they're not and undervalue what they are."
> —Malcolm Forbes

words, that's for sure. Look at the first quote in the box again. I think of that old saying "Appearances can be deceiving." If we don't honestly admit to our weaknesses, we can have the "artifice of strength," but not real, lasting strength. We always know we're lying to ourselves.

We need to know our weaknesses as much as we need to know our strengths because if we aren't honest about our weaknesses we're probably not going to be honest about our strengths and we're not going to know which areas to focus on transferring our strengths to. Being honest means both admitting to our weaknesses (which most of us can do) and not exaggerating those weaknesses out of a twisted sense of modesty. Most of us have been taught not to toot our own horn, so we say how bad we are at this, that, or the other when it isn't true.

We find it easy to cheer on our children, spouses, coworkers, friends, and families, to tell them they're good at *x*, *y*, or *z* (not to mention consoling them when they're not so good at other things). But when it comes to admitting and yes, even praising ourselves for the individual qualities or skills we possess, a critical voice in our head begins just about every thought in that direction with *Yes, but . . . Yes, but it's immodest to say I'm good at . . . Yes, but I'm not really so good at . . . Yes, but, other people do it better. . . .* Even when we can state what we're good at, the tendency to compare ourselves with others can throw us off. Recognize the following scenario? You can admit you're basically capable, your house isn't in a total shambles, you earn praise at work, and your family is functioning, if not reasonably happy. But one of the women in your carpool group not only has a spotless house, over-achieving children, and a thriving business, she coordinates neighbor-hood activities, irons her kids' T-shirts, bakes all her family's bread, and designs her own outfits. Next to her, you feel inadequate, and all your abilities seem insignificant.

Boy, do I understand. For a long time I was on a one-woman crusade to become, if not *the* perfect homemaker, mother, and career woman, then at least a candidate. I attended seminars that were supposed to help me organize my home and manage my time better. I usually came away glowing with inspiration. I would buy each expert's philosophy hook, line, and sinker, sometimes along with a boatload of materials that would make it a snap to organize our schedules and demands. I think the longest the glow ever lasted was about eighteen hours. Then feel-ings of guilt and inadequacy set in. What was wrong with me? How could hundreds of thousands of women have time to make their homes perfect havens, their offices organized and smooth-running, and I couldn't get dinner on the table at a decent hour?

I have never been one to give up easily. Bound and determined to get this home-and-family thing down, I watched different friends balance dual careers, figuring I could pick up skills and techniques by imitation and osmosis. I tried to be like them, which made me feel even worse about myself. I pretty much stopped doing that after I stacked myself up against my friend Susan, the one who after working a ten-hour day fixes beef Wellington for dinner and a Sacher torte for dessert; organizes flow charts for her family's activities for a year at a time; can locate the owner's manual for her ten-year-old blender; and knows the birthdays and anniversaries of

> I am not hundreds of thousands of other women.

all her clients, her boss's favorite color and clothes sizes, and the agendas for the next seven staff meetings. She also has a master's in home economics and a bachelor's in office management.

Susan was my undoing. Next to her I felt like a simpleton. Eventually I realized that we can never really see the whole picture of someone else's life. In my initial admiration of Susan I didn't register her frenziedness and lack of enjoyment of any of the areas she excels in. Perhaps I have accomplished a bit less, but I do feel a measure of satisfaction with what I've done.

That was when I also understood that I should give myself pretty high marks as a person who knows how to get people to buy into an idea or one who knows how to plan fun occasions with Bill and the boys. The day I realized this was the day I realized I could, for example, plan a terrific party at my house or anywhere else. I didn't have to compare my party—decorations, party setup, or hors d'oeuvres—to my friend's. I could finally acknowledge the fact that people like coming to our home because it's ours, not because they're expecting four-star food and avant-garde decorating. In fact, they like visiting *because* our furniture is comfortable and the atmosphere is welcoming. And I've learned to ask Bill to help a lot with the cooking for parties (which he is happy to do) or pick up hors d'oeuvres at the local deli.

Being a person who enjoys life and feels a sense of accomplishment doesn't show up on lists of skills, but it's an enormously important aspect of life. And comparing yourself with others is a good way to lose your pleasure in life. The thing is, comparing does no one any good. It creates and perpetuates discouragement. Stop comparing—now.

> "Comparisons are odorous."
> —William Shakespeare
>
> "Couples who cook together stay together. (Maybe because they can't decide who'll get the Cuisinart.)" —Erica Jong

> Stop comparing—now.

Start Counting

Start *really* counting what you're good at. Even if we're people who do feel a certain sense of accomplishment, given the hectic nature of our lives in this culture, given the constant urge to push on for more or better, we often don't take the time to list our accomplishments and savor them.

Accomplishments are accomplishments whether they're things we have to do regularly, like the laundry or quarterly sales reports at work, or things we've been working on for a long time, like losing forty pounds or organizing your company's move to a new office. You might have hosted an open house months ago that your friends still talk about. You

---

Your Own Top Ten

I, _____, on this _____ day of _____ in the year _____ do hereby certify that I have accomplished these ten wonderful things:

1.

2.

3.

4.

5.

6.

7.

8.

9.

10.

Congratulations to me!

might have mounted photos you've been storing in boxes into albums for your children. You might simply have gotten through a difficult day in which five people needed to be in seven different places at overlapping times. Or you might have done something unusual and different, like taking a Spanish class, getting a promotion, or organizing and executing a family grounds maintenance day. Whatever it is, it is an accomplishment.

Transferring Skills

You may be saying, "Okay, I understand I'm a uniquely gifted individual. I'm even happy about the abilities I have. But what about the areas I'm not so skillful in? Even if I don't compare myself with Shiny Sally down the block, I know there are things I don't handle well. What can I do about those?"

First, know that you're not alone. In talking with countless women across the country I've found that most of them feel very good about their performance in two of the family management departments and completely inadequate in two of them; the other three they're okay with. This is certainly true of me. Just ask my family or my banker. They encourage me regularly to keep learning in the food and finance departments, which I do. And although I'm no Julia Child and I don't belong to the Beardstown ladies' investment group, I'm making progress. And the way I'm doing it is by adapting and applying my strengths—my core competencies—to these areas of weakness.

For example, in the kitchen I compensate for my weakness with a strength: presentation. As I mentioned earlier, I worked at my mother's store while I was growing up, and there I learned a lot about display techniques. Early on I realized that not only do I have a preference for a cheery milieu, but I have a knack for creating it (aha!

> "Build on your strengths and your weaknesses will be irrelevant." —Peter Drucker

something to feel good about!). That helps me in my work when I'm shooting a video and decorating the set, or thinking of ideas for the layout of a book or magazine article. Experience has shown me I have an eye for color, style, and balance, and I understand how the power of presentation can transform the ordinary or less-than-perfect (most of my meals fall someplace in between) into the appealing.

Think about it. Nowhere is this power more evident than in the restaurant business. I decided to start taking notes—learning from the experts—while eating out. Have you ever wondered why ordinary pasta (which probably came from a box just like the one I use at home) seems like a culinary masterpiece at an Italian restaurant? It might be the homemade sauce that simmered for three days, but it's also the extra panache: the freshly ground pepper, the bright-colored pasta bowl, the checkered tablecloth, the single flower, and the candles. This is, as the French say, ambiance, and that special-occasion feeling doesn't have to be limited to experiences in fine restaurants.

I can't serve pasta with slave-all-day-for-it homemade sauce, but I can serve my from-the-jar sauce and box pasta on a handmade pottery platter, using pretty bowls and colorful plates. I can try to orchestrate meaningful, fun conversation at the table by drawing each family member out about his or her day and by talking about what we've been doing or reading. I can let candlelight and music smooth the rough edges of the day. In short, I can put my best foot forward in an area where I feel extremely challenged.

Our areas of incompetency offer opportunities for us to use some of our strengths toward turning around those weak areas. Recently I read an article in the *Wall Street Journal* about women executives rising to the top. Women who have broken through the glass ceiling, the article reports, have something remarkable in common, aside from their intellectual skills, marketing and motivational abilities, and willingness to take risks and work hard. At some point in their careers, they took over troubled departments—in many cases, departments about which the women knew little and for which they had limited training—and turned them around. They used their skills to reengineer the floundering departments and made them successful.

> "There is only one woman I know of who could never be a symphony conductor, and that's the Venus de Milo."
> —Margaret Hillis

Think about that for a moment. Which departments are floundering in your Family Management concern? Why is that? Is it really because you're a terrible cook? Congenitally tardy? Kill houseplants at alarming rates? Or is it because you haven't yet figured out how to apply your strengths to the department at hand?

The women described in the article saw opportunities where others saw problems. They were also willing to risk applying their strengths to areas that were weak in their companies.

Knowing your strengths and your weaknesses is the first step to using your skills more effectively. Then it's a matter of regularly patting yourself on the back for accomplishments. Here are four strategies I've used—and seen lots of others use—to expand my areas of strength and minimize my weaknesses:

Three-way Win

Consider your core competencies when volunteering at your child's school. If you are creative, volunteer to decorate the classroom for the holidays. Let your child help you. If you're organized, you can coordinate the candy-bar fund-raiser. An older child can help keep records and make phone calls. Or, if you're a people person, run a booth at the fall carnival. Whatever you do, volunteer for projects you can do at home or on the weekends—and always with your kids. Not only are you doing something you enjoy, your kids are learning the value of volunteering, and you're spending time together.

1. Develop Your Competitive Edge

You do this at work—why not at home? The Japanese, who are big on competition, use the term *kaisen*, which means constant incremental improvement. No, no one will ever be good at everything, but yes, everyone can learn new skills or improve on her existing ones. What do you want to get better at doing? How could you do it? Is there a class you could take? Will practice help? Is there someone you could ask to teach you how he or she does something? Is it a matter of figuring out how to do things you don't particularly like to do, like housework?

I know a woman who loves to keep in motion, intellectually and physically. Sometimes she feels like her performance in the Home and Property area, particularly in terms of daily maintenance, suffers. She's an at-home entrepreneur with a flexible schedule and at least four balls up in the air at once. She loves to get a lot done. Quantity pleases her. So she decided to look at her ability to keep her house clean the way a runner might improve by shaving time off her pace. When this woman takes a break, she measures how many stray pieces of paper, coats, and pairs of shoes she can put away in five minutes. She's discovered she can clean a toilet and a sink in five minutes. Three five-minute breaks and she's got the bathroom cleaned. Five more minutes and the dishwasher is emptied. Five more minutes and there's a load of laundry in the washer and another in the dryer. For this woman, improving her competitive edge wasn't about sitting down and figuring out how to keep her house clean. It wasn't about adding more tasks in this area to her daily Hit List. She'd tried that and she simply didn't do the things related to cleaning. For her it was the satisfaction of spending less time doing more things, getting faster and faster.

Delegation is a good area in which to develop a competitive edge. Watch masters at work. Ask a friend or coworker to share her techniques. Be creative. For instance, a woman who takes a writing class to improve her written communications skills at work might discover that a side benefit of the class is learning to state explicitly what she needs or desires. That skill is, of course, eminently transferable to delegating. We can't delegate unless we can say specifically what it is we need or want the other person to do.

> "The illiterate of the future will not be the person who cannot read. It will be the person who does not know how to learn."
> —Alvin Toffler

Competitive edges can be about doing more, doing things faster, doing them better, or learning new skills that complement the ones you already have. Doing things better doesn't necessarily mean doing them perfectly or even at the 98 percent level. Sometimes, paradoxically, doing things better can mean lowering your standards. Say you're comparing yourself with your mother, the one whose floor you could literally eat off of. Maybe she set your standard of a clean house. In your job you probably have learned about return on investment. You would never ask your company to commit time and money to a project that wouldn't provide a return on investment. Maybe you need to lower your standards to a place where you're comfortable with the return on investment.

2. Compensate for Your Weak Points

When possible, delegate the task to someone more skilled at it than you are. This indicates not your weakness in that area but your strength as a leader. A good leader gets the job done in the best way possible. If that means you need to get someone else to do it, you're wise to take advantage of his or her talent (see Chapter 5 on delegating and communicating). I would just remind you that by delegating, you're not just developing your skills as a leader and Family Manager; you're also doing your children a big favor by teaching them the value of cooperation in creating a home you can all live in comfortably and letting them practice skills they'll need for their adult lives.

You may be able to overpower your particular weakness with one or more of your strengths. If you've ever played tennis, you know that there are ways to compensate for a weak backhand. You can take lessons that concentrate on improving your backhand. You can position yourself on the court so that you don't have to use it as often. You can develop a fast, harder-to-return serve so your opponent doesn't put you in the position of having to return a ball with a backhand. You can develop an attitude so your opponent doesn't immediately see that you have a weak backhand. You will, in fact, probably do all of these things, maybe even without realizing it.

In the Family Management arena, if you have a weak backhand in, say, the financial area, you can take a money-management seminar. You can delegate by paying a college student who is majoring in accounting to reconcile your bank statements. Or you can overpower your weakness: use your strength at organization so that you have everything in place to pay bills on time. Use your strength at rewarding yourself for a job well done by making sure that you have a favorite treat after you finish financial tasks. Use your strength at creating a good ambiance by setting up an area where you work on finances, a setting with pictures and surroundings that please you and with all the tools you need—pens, envelopes, paper, stamps, a record book—to get the job done. Use your research skills to find a bank that will automatically pay your monthly bills for little or no fee or to investigate how to get the best possible bang for your buck in large and small purchases. Use your advance-planning skills by purchasing canned drinks when they're on sale for the Fourth of July even though the baseball-team party isn't until August, by buying clothes at end-of-season sales, by knowing you'll need something six months from now and getting it while it's on sale. This could be anything from an air conditioner in November to an overcoat in May.

3. Adapt Your Strengths

Concentrate on what you're good at and aggressively look for ways to adapt those

> "Don't find fault; find a remedy." —Henry Ford

Ten Compensating Strategies

The idea is to replace what you're not good at or don't like doing with something you are good at or enjoy. These strategies are about buying, bartering, or hiring as well as delegation and communication. Use those ideas that apply to your life, and draw on them to come up with your own.

1. Trade with a friend. She organizes your filing system and you plant her garden.
2. Put the teenager who loves to drive in charge of getting the car in for repairs.
3. Find a dentist who will call you to remind you of checkup times.
4. If you can't deal with clutter but can't stop accumulating it, put attractive catchall boxes in strategic places—the family room, the kitchen, your bedroom. Deal with them when they get full.
5. Buy fancy desserts and appetizers if you're not a good cook.
6. Make an accountability pact with your husband. Agree to remind each other, in a nice way, to do unpleasant tasks you both have to do.
7. Don't stew in your own juices. Make a deal with a friend to call each other when you're feeling incompetent.
8. Buy clothes that don't need to be ironed if you're no good at ironing or hate to do it.
9. Take on an extra project and earn enough money to hire someone to do your spring yard work.
10. If you like to exercise but can't seem to make the time, set a standing date with a friend to meet you at the gym.

skills in other areas. A woman I met recently after a Family Manager seminar told me she used to be president of a company. She resigned her position when she had a baby to be home full time. It wasn't long before she felt very frustrated. Housekeeping was not her gift. "I couldn't understand why," she said, "I could run a company, but not my home." She told me that the principles she learned at the Family Manager seminar made a lightbulb come on. "Of course!" she said with relief, "I simply need to adapt the skills I used to make the company successful to my home." She knew she could approach managing her home from this new perspective and be successful.

Even as I'm writing this chapter I've figured out a way to lessen my own frustration. If you came to my house and opened up my kitchen cupboards, pantry, drawers, or refrigerator, you'd find them fairly neat and organized. But open up my freezer and prepare to have something fall on your toe. The frozen foods are always messily stashed in whatever space is available on the freezer shelves. Trust me when I say this is not inspirational when I'm trying to figure out what to cook for dinner. I can hardly tell what's in there, or at least I couldn't until last week. It occurred to me that I am good at categorizing and organizing information, a skill I use in my writing. Why couldn't I then, I asked myself, categorize and organize the frozen foods in the same way I file ideas for child raising, time management, home maintenance, and holidays? This may sound elementary to some of you, but it was a big deal to me. I even labeled the shelves in my freezer—breads, meats, vegetables, and desserts and juices—the same way I label files, and I enjoyed doing it, even though I was in the kitchen!

Here's a list of possible skills that can be transferred from your outside career to your Family Management career, and skills that can be transferred from one Family Management department to another. Use this as a starting place. Go back to your own strengths and think about how you can transfer them.

IF YOU CAN	YOU CAN
organize files	keep records, warranties, instruction manuals accessible and up to date.
use your time well at work	figure out how to do it at home.
juggle three projects at work	do it at home, thinking in terms of projects instead of distasteful tasks.
sell a product well	sell your family on the idea of pitching in.
follow complex recipes	follow complex assembly instructions. (Simply think about how you learned to break the recipe down into step-by-step increments and do the same thing.)
plan for the release of a new product a year ahead	plan ahead for special projects—for example, holidays or a family reunion.
assemble all the supplies a classroom of kids need for a creative art project	assemble all the supplies you need to prepare a creative dinner project.
create a pleasant dining ambiance	create a pleasant bill-paying or laundry ambiance.
think of creative ways to play	think of creative ways to work.
research new technology at work	research the purchase of a new microwave.
make sure your kids are eating right and getting exercise	make sure you are eating right and getting exercise.
read professional journals that inspire you at the office	read books that inspire you in your emotional and spiritual life.
lead a task force to finish a project at the office	lead your family task force to finish a project at home.

4. Learn to Cope with Incompetencies

The key to coping with your incompetencies is to emphasize the areas you excel in. Then find something you like about the areas you don't excel in and focus your energy on that. If a big priority for you is friends and family, but throwing birthday parties and holiday gatherings causes you to overdose on antacids, do what you can instead. Be a person who finds unique ways to celebrate special days and people. Instead of pushing yourself to organize a big party or plan a sit-down dinner, consider spur-of-the-moment potlucks. Or when you have a free evening, ask another family over for a simple dessert and to watch a movie. Or make a grocery shopping date with a friend. You can go for coffee first or afterward if you have a cooler in your car for perishable items and thereby make a mini-occasion out of a chore you both have to do anyway. I know one woman who has had a standing Christmas shopping date with the same friend for more than ten years. They both have those hard-to-buy-for people on their list—doesn't everyone? Over the years they've gotten to know each other's. They offer each other creative suggestions. They give each other honest feedback, preventing that last-minute-it-costs-too-much-but-I've-got-to-get-something syndrome. And they have fun. They chat while they walk from store to store and drive from place to place.

The point is, the skills you use when you are enjoying yourself the most—in your work, in your home, or when you are doing some hobby or recreation—are transferable to other tasks.

Once you've done all you can with the skills you already have, consider how you might improve in the areas you're not as talented in. There's no law that says you're stuck with what nature gave you; everyone can learn. This doesn't mean you'll become equally comfortable in all of the seven departments; you'll probably always feel a little inadequate in certain

> "Being able to do something well is one of life's great joys."
> —Frank Tyger

areas. This is perfectly all right! No one is great at *everything*. Besides, I've found that our learning most often occurs in areas we're not comfortable in, because

then we know we need the help and we're eager to get it. If you're a good seamstress, you might decide to learn to build shelves. Making things is making things, whether out of cloth or wood. If you're long on energy but short on ability when it comes to taking care of your vehicle, you might take a basic mechanics course at your local community college. Your passion to do better will glean equally strong results.

Be Flexible

I recently spent an afternoon with my friend Dr. Kathryn Waldrep. She shared something about her work with me that I've never realized before. When she begins an operation, she always knows what the outcome or goal is. It could be delivering a baby or removing an ovarian cyst. She has the skills to do the job, but she has to be flexible. "Each woman's body is different," she told me, "and I never know exactly what my approach is going to be until I see what the situation is." I thought about the fact that we should operate with the same kind of flexibility when using any of our skills. Instead of getting flustered when we've planned out how the evening schedule should run and our family isn't cooperating, maybe we can be flexible when dinner, homework, chores, and family time happen. Just so the end goal—kids in bed at nine—is reached.

We all have short- and long-term goals that we're not entirely sure how to reach until we get started toward them. When we're redecorating a room, for instance, we may know what effect we want—a pleasant, light room that won't be hard to clean. But there are other considerations, cost often among them. When a friend of mine was redoing her living room, she looked into new window treatments for her

> "Ignore people who say it can't
> be done."   —Elaine Rideout

large French windows. She was aston-
ished at the quotes she got. Then one day
while she was shopping for something
else she came across inexpensive room divider screens. *Aha,* she thought,
window coverings don't have to be on the window. Now she has two
white screens standing in front of her windows. They can be folded
and moved aside. They prevent people from seeing in, but they also let
in light. And they were a third the cost of the cheapest of the other
alternatives.

Go Ahead—Enjoy Yourself!

Above all, revel in the aptitudes you're blessed with. Go ahead and
enjoy the things you're good at—to the max—and don't let others ne-
gate them. All of us are multitalented, and we should celebrate those
strengths by using them as much as possible. I feel my greatest joy when
I am busily using the gifts I've been given.

You don't have to prove you're smart and capable—that's a given.
You need reach only for whatever improvement you can make and all
the enjoyment you can stand!

Smart Strategy

Balancing two full-time jobs demands a set of skills that no one person has. There
will always be jobs you hate. The trick is learning to work with your strengths,
around the areas where you are not gifted, and through people who are.

Keeping Your Balance

- Your competence as a Family Manager is already established.
- Identify—and own—the things you're good at. Be your own cheerleader.
- Acknowledge, but don't be consumed by, your weaknesses. The best of us have them.
- View areas of incompetency as opportunities, not obstacles.
- In both of your careers, stay competitive in a healthy way.
- Emphasize the areas you excel in.
- Enjoy and use your abilities to the maximum!

EIGHT
Turn Roadblocks into Building Blocks

"Life is a grindstone. But whether it grinds us down or polishes us
up depends on us."   —L. Thomas Holdcroft

As I reflect on our twenty-six years of family life, I see a lot of
wonderful pictures in my mind's eye: refurbishing old furniture
on Saturdays; playing in family Spades tournaments—the Blondes
vs. the Brunettes—until the wee hours of the morning; everyone laughing at my snow-skiing catastrophes; picnicking and flying kites at the
park; delivering litters of puppies together. I also see the stress-filled
times: sick children, surgeries, financial calamities, painful relationships,
undeserved and deserved criticism, broken appliances and cars, out-
bursts of anger, accidents.

Although it was almost a year ago, it seems like yesterday that Joel
and I left Nashville before dawn to drive to Waco, Texas, where he
would enter Baylor University as a freshman. We stopped in Dallas to
pick up a rental car at the airport so, after leaving him with his car in
Waco, I could drive back to Dallas, attend a publishing meeting, then
catch a plane home to Nashville.

As Joel followed me on the interstate during the last leg of our trip,
we ran into rain—heavy, blinding rain. I slowed down and strained
to see his car in my rearview mirror. I finally saw his headlights approaching. Then in horror I watched his car career out of control,

swerving all over the highway. A split second later I saw it dive over a guardrail and into a field. My heart raced as I tried to keep my own car under control. I pulled off the road, turned my car around in the grass, and drove back through the field to find him.

> "Not to have had pain is not to have been human."
> —Jewish proverb
>
> "I force myself to laugh at everything for fear of being obliged to weep."
> —Pierre-Augustin de Beaumarchais

Thankfully, Joel's car landed upright. He was shaken up, but not hurt. It was scary, and when my mind replays that roadside scene, I can't help but think that's a picture of the way many of us feel sometimes. We're traveling through life, trying to steer our lives and our families in a positive direction, but then all of a sudden we're swerving out of control. Unexpected problems interrupt our plans and our lives and leave us shaken.

Some of the problems we encounter are relatively small (although they don't seem small at the time) and can be fairly easily dealt with. They go from catastrophe to family joke in no time flat. My recipe for turkey in a pastry shell falls into that category. If you've never tried to wrap a twenty-pound turkey in a snug pastry shell, trust me, you don't want to give it a whirl. And at two on Thanksgiving afternoon, when twenty people are ready to sit down to eat and the pastry crust is black on the outside and the turkey is red on the inside, it can seem like a disaster on the order of a hundred-year flood. But it's not. And turning it into a funny family story, with a lesson for everyone, isn't that hard either. In this case, I now follow a gourmet-cook friend's rule for Thanksgiving: Keep it simple and traditional. Ever since my tom turkey masqueraded as an overgrown doughboy, I've followed that advice.

But we all know other times when it's not so simple, when the situation is serious, when there's nothing to laugh about. There is no easy or obvious lesson when we're faced with loss of a home, a job, someone we love; when we have a sick child or must endure pain and suffering. We are human. We can't understand why some things happen to us. We can't understand why after we work so hard and feel we deserve a break, someone else who seemingly doesn't lift a finger is showered with blessings.

I'm not a psychologist or a therapist. And I'd be the first person to suggest that when you have overwhelming problems, when life throws you a curve, seeking help from qualified people is a very good idea. Talking with a counselor can ease the pain and provide new insights into handling problems. Sometimes we need the help of experts. Few of us hesitate to see a physician when we're ill. To my mind, asking a counselor for help through an emotional crisis, seeking the guidance of a spiritual adviser in a crisis of faith, or getting the advice of a financial counselor for extreme money difficulties or a career counselor for problems at work is only reasonable.

This chapter is about troubleshooting—how to deal with the problems we can do something about, those that hinder, say, our family mission or personal goals. Maybe it's a bad situation that keeps recurring or perhaps a disappointment that makes our day—and our personality—go from bad to worse. It could be something as small as an interruption that keeps us from getting through our daily Hit List. What are the things we can change, and how do we do it?

Reacting and Responding

First and foremost, we must learn to respond instead of react. When we react—act on our first impulse, usually out of anger or frustration—we often cause ourselves and others more trouble. We simply need to take the time to think through how to solve the problem that's confronting us. We've probably all been in the situation where we hit the panic button and get ourselves stuck in the elevator. It can happen so easily. I've done it myself when an editor asked me for minor

> "By choosing your response to life experiences, you choose your result."
> —Dr. Eric Allenbaugh

changes in a magazine article. I didn't
register the part about a small problem
that a few small revisions in the introduc-

> "Anger is a brief madness."
> —Horace

tion and conclusion would solve. Instead, I reacted. How could she not
like it? I worked so long on it. *She hates my work,* I thought. *She hates
me. She'll never ask me to write anything for her again.* Then I got angry
at her for not understanding my work. And I immediately began to
rearrange my schedule to find another fifteen hours between now and
the day after tomorrow to rewrite the whole thing. All I really needed to
do was to talk with her some more, pinpoint the exact problems, and
spend half an hour or so fixing them. And I could have done that if I'd
taken the time to listen carefully, think, and respond.

Another thing I'm pretty good at is putting problems through the
enlarging machine in my mind (and although you won't find a picture of
one in medical books, we all seem to have one). I've found the enlarging
machine operates at all hours of the day, but it seems to be most active
at night. That's when we lie awake reviewing situations like one lost
client. Somehow we move from a fairly insignificant occurrence to
scenes from a soap opera: We are never going to work in our profession
again. We're going to go broke, lose the house, or use up all our retirement savings. When we're working the enlarging machine, the last thing
we think of doing is responding creatively by going out and finding a
new client, or calling on the one we lost to see if there's a possibility of
a turnabout.

Or we go over and over our child's hurt feelings on the soccer field or
in dance class. He or she is marred for life, we assume, and will never
learn to play team sports or enjoy dancing, will never try anything new
again, will never get into a good college. Or you name it . . .

Another way to react is to close up and refuse to deal with the
problem. This often happens, again, after we've put a smallish sort of
problem into the enlarger and blown it way out of proportion. We've
lost one sale, our career is doomed, and there's nothing we can do about

> The problem with a reactive approach to any kind of problem is that it doesn't solve the problem.

it, so we won't do anything. This reaction is close kin to the it'll-go-away-if-I-ignore-it technique of problem solving. And that's close kin to the it's-not-a-problem-if-I-say-it's-not-a-problem approach. There is a problem if a three-year-old is hitting other kids in her play group. And no amount of "Isn't she cute? It's just a stage; kids will be kids" is going to teach her that it's not okay behavior. I'm not saying that a kid who hits other kids in preschool will automatically grow up to be an ax murderer. Chances are she won't. But if we don't respond to the problem, chances are she also won't learn the skills she needs to get along with other people in life. The problem with a reactive approach to any kind of problem is that it doesn't solve the problem.

I sometimes think that reacting to problems is being built into our psyches. Most of us have grown up with television. We expect life to be like thirty minutes of a situation comedy. There are three acts, broken up by commercials, and the characters all live happily ever after. We all make fun of it. We all say, "Oh, no, not me. I don't really expect that." But we continue to react to problems in our own lives as if there were a quick fix, one-time, cure-all solution. And we move on to bigger problems. Or we run them through the enlarger. Or we stick our heads in the sand. Or we run away from them.

Responding is a different kettle of fish. Responding is a slower process. It demands that we listen carefully, that we examine and often adjust our attitude, and that we calmly look at possible approaches to solving the problem before we take action.

Attitude

> "It is a characteristic of wisdom not to do desperate things." —Henry David Thoreau

As surely as day follows night, you, I, and our families can grow stronger during hard times. Nobody likes to experience pain. Only masochists seek it out. Yet there is pain in every life. There's no escaping it. So we have two choices. We can try to avoid pain by avoiding doing anything that's difficult for us, by refusing to participate in life. Or we can learn to face our pain and try to solve our problems. Avoiding pain guarantees a shallow life. Facing pain and seeking to grow from it develop character.

In order to do this, we must be tenacious. But unfortunately this isn't a quality we have often seen in action. We're accustomed to one-hour photo processing and ten-minute lube jobs; if something isn't microwavable, we think hard about whether it's worth cooking. We're the instant generation and we want our problems to be worked out thus—instantly. And when they're not, we want to bolt, change anything—jobs, husbands, kids, locations, houses. We don't like pain, and we don't like to patiently work through problems.

I've found that the problems from which I would like to escape are the very things I grow from dealing with. If my goal is the immediate relief of pain, then bailing out makes a lot of sense, as does heroin. If, however, I want to see the bigger picture, I must realize that painful situations are part of life's never-ending curriculum for me. Maybe I can learn to endure hard times a little bit—to know deep inside that they are temporary and will prove to be valuable somehow.

My attitude in a difficult situation cannot be blamed on that situation or on someone else. The older I get, the more I realize how little control I have over life's circumstances—and other people. But I *do* have control over what I choose to focus on, and that greatly affects my attitude and my ability to solve the problem.

> "With the right attitude, all the problems in the world will not make you a failure. With the wrong mental attitude, all the help in the world will not make you a success."
> —Warren Deaton

> "Instead of changing addresses, address the issue."
> —Dr. Eric Allenbaugh

> "When I enter into my pain rather than run from it, I will find at the center of my pain an amazing insight."—John Powell

"The greater part of our happiness or misery depends on our dispositions, and not on our circumstances. We carry the seeds of the one or the other about with us . . . wherever we go."
—Martha Washington

"Think of it as being easy, and it shall be easy. Think of it as being difficult, and it shall be difficult."   —Arabian proverb

"Adversity reveals genius, prosperity conceals it."
—Horace

This last holiday season, I realized I could take attitude lessons from my father. As arthritis has slowly but deliberately crippled him over the past thirty-five years, I have never heard him complain. Even when he was obviously in pain and having difficulty walking, he made the trip to our house and said how glad he was to be there. He believes it is unproductive to wallow in his problems. He doesn't waste time on the dead-end belief that he deserves to be able to run up five flights of stairs. Instead, he is thankful that he can walk at all and makes the most of his life.

In every problem we face, we have a choice as to what to focus on. I want to be like my father—able to focus on what's right, not fixate on what's wrong. I'm not talking about being Pollyannaish, about not being honest, about sugarcoating problems. That is a form of reacting, not responding reasonably. I'm talking about going into the problem realizing that there is something I can do and some good can come of it.

Last Tuesday at our house/office, we were in phone hell. Both of our telephone lines suddenly went out, which means our fax machine was down and we couldn't send or receive e-mail. Of course this was the busiest day of the year. I was having a hard time believing something good could come out of it. I needed access to the world—now! I was in react mode, with a bad attitude. I told Bill we should call the phone company. Instead, Bill, alias Mr. Why Pay Someone Else to Fix It?, decided to crawl under the house to see what he could do. My frustration mounted. After all, what good can come of stubborn phones and a stubborn husband? Well, he didn't fix the phone lines. But once he was under the house, he found a hot water pipe that had burst and was leaking all over the place. I don't know how long it would have taken us to discover the leak, how much damage it would have done, and how much it would have cost to fix it—a lot, I suspect—if he hadn't gone down there. And even though we had to call the phone company *and* the plumber, I'm sure glad he did what he did.

When I'm having trouble with my attitude, I've often wished for a place where I could get an attitude overhaul—a place like my local garage, where I could take

> "Peace is not the absence of conflict from life, but the ability to cope with it."
> —Anonymous
>
> "You are 100 percent responsible for your own happiness. Other people aren't responsible. Your parents aren't responsible. Your spouse isn't. You alone are. So if you are not happy, it's up to you to change something. It's not up to someone else to 'fix it' for you."   —Dr. Gerald D. Bell

myself and someone would painlessly do the necessary adjustments and replacements in a few hours. I could pay them and come home good as new. The truth is it usually takes more than a few hours, and it's not something that can be done to us; it must be done by us.

One thing I've found is that it helps to have someone to hold you accountable for your attitude. I have two friends who do that for me. They gently and firmly call me on the carpet when I'm being unnecessarily negative or critical. I do the same for them.

In a family, when you're dealing with a problem, a positive perspective has incredible interpersonal effects. It looks for the good. It eliminates the necessity of critical remarks and manipulative behavior on my part. Since these tactics don't work anyway, I do myself and others a favor when I give up my compulsion to concentrate on what's wrong and my desire to blame everyone else and simply focus on my attitude.

> "There is always a better way."
> —Thomas Edison

Approach

A number of years ago when I was going through a particularly hard time, I had a pretty good attitude, but I didn't know what to do about the problem. It seemed overwhelming and I couldn't figure out how to work it out. A friend shared this riddle with me: When is a horse like a violin? The answer is, Only when you're high above the horse. Think about it. If you look down at it, it doesn't look like a horse. It looks like the shape of a violin. She was telling me to get a new perspective on the problem, to look at it from a different angle. When we do that, we often begin to see how to solve problems.

When I first stepped out on my dream to write books that would help busy women strengthen their families, I didn't have a publisher. Not only that, I had never taken a writing class. I hadn't written anything but personal journals since college days. These seemed like huge problems that threatened my dream to write. I decided to look at the problems from several different angles and do what I could. I started reading books, lots of books, by excellent writers, and I made notes about their styles. I read texts and manuals on how to write and I signed up for a writing class at a local college. Then another problem appeared (or didn't appear): money. A friend and I self-published the first book on a

---

Questions You Can Ask Yourself for an Attitude Tune-up

1. What's my part in the argument? How is my attitude keeping the fight going?
2. In any given problem situation, how do I see the glass as half empty? How do I see it as half full?
3. Am I completely comfortable with my own behavior in x, y, or z situation? What attitude produces that behavior?
4. As an advertising slogan of some years ago went, Where's the beef? What exactly is my problem with this problem?

budget of only $2,000, so we could print only 1,000 copies. We had no money for advertising, so we had to attack the problem from a different angle: Instead of thinking what we couldn't do because we didn't have the money, we thought about what we could do that didn't cost much. We went to the public library and looked up on microfiche the yellow pages bookstore ads for fifteen large cities. Then we sent a copy of our book and a cover letter to the bookstores, asking them to buy the book. A week or so later I called the bookstores and asked if they would buy our book. Most did. Writing letters doesn't cost much, so I wrote letters and sent a book to the national morning shows and to CNN. Then I called them back and, miraculously, I found the person at CNN who had seen our book. I talked her into sending a crew to our house to do a story. The rest is history. Even though the lack of writing know-how and money were big problems, a little creative thinking and looking at the problems from different angles turned them into opportunities.

PROBLEM: You don't have enough time to make dressing from scratch (using your grandmother's recipe, of course) for Thanksgiving.
Look at it from your family's perspective. How bad would it be if you ordered some stuffing from a restaurant and picked it up Wednesday afternoon? Wouldn't they rather see you relaxed than overreacting? (Or see if one of your budding chefs would like to make it. With a little luck you might delegate this job for good.)

PROBLEM: You never see your best friend anymore.
Look at it from the perspective of things you both have to do. Are there errands you can do together?

PROBLEM: Your babysitter falls through at the last minute and you can't find another.
Look at it as an opportunity. Do something fun with the whole family instead of just your husband. Or check your address book. Call and offer to exchange babysitting time with a neighborhood friend.

PROBLEM: You have trouble keeping one particular area of your house clean, like the bathroom.

Look at it from the point of view of the number of times you use it in a day. Do one small cleaning task every time you use it.

PROBLEM: You have a number of large items you want to get rid of but you don't want to have a garage sale and you don't have the means to get them hauled away.

Look in the yellow pages. Find a charitable organization that picks things up.

PROBLEM: You're at your wits' end with a four-year-old whiner.

Look to your friends with children a bit older. Ask for ideas.

PROBLEM: You've been feeling like you don't have enough of anything.

Look at this problem from the point of view of assets. How can you use them?

IDENTIFY THE ROADBLOCKS

Some automobile and travel clubs provide a great service for members who are taking road trips. Not only will they give you maps, but they will also give you up-to-date information on detours and road construction, places you may expect delays, and alternate routes. As we approach our problems from different angles, we need to figure out where the road-blocks are and how to deal with them. The goal is to turn roadblocks into building blocks.

The first step to turning roadblocks into building blocks is to iden-tify what your roadblocks are. Consider the following categories as you assess the roadblocks in your life. Make a list of the ones that particularly plague you, with a specific example from your life. Label each one as actual, probable, or potential—don't be pessi-

> "Nothing will ever be attempted if all possible objections must be first overcome." —Samuel Johnson

mistic. Then think about and list possible different techniques for dealing with them.

1. *We're too busy.* This is probably the biggest problem for every dual-career woman. If our calendars are filled until eternity, if we never take time to stop and think, if we're always responding to interruptions and distractions that call for more attention than they deserve, we'll very likely never change things much for the better.

We need to learn to view our schedules and time from a different angle. One way is to look for bits of time to accomplish tasks a little at a time. There are only twenty-four hours in every day. Time is a built-in constraint that we must accept. The fact is, we will never have enough time to do everything we dream of doing. That's what focus and setting priorities are for. It is possible, however, to be so busy with the details of life that we don't have time to do the most important things. Some ruthless assessment of our schedules is in order for most of us:

Are you always overbooked?

Do you have a master calendar?

Do you make decisions based on what other people want you to do rather than on what you want to do?

Do you make decisions on how to use your time based on what's good for your family or on what your boss expects?

There's an old adage that if you want to get something done, ask a busy person. And to a certain extent, that's true. Women with two full-time jobs are people who know how to get things done. On the other hand, a person can follow through on all the plans in the world, but without solid priorities behind her, not much of lasting benefit is likely to happen.

> "Whenever decisions are made strictly on the basis of bottom-line arithmetic, human beings get crunched along with the numbers." —Thomas R. Horton

2. *We're tired.* Former football coach Vince Lombardi was right when he said,

"Fatigue makes cowards of us all." If we're drained, depressed, or just plain tired, chances are we won't be able to envision what we want our personal and professional lives to look like. Creatively solving problems takes energy. If we don't take time to take care of ourselves, if we don't schedule times of rest and refreshment into our lives, we won't have the energy we need. I have a friend who does get a lot done. She's employed at a furniture store and goes to school full time. A single parent, she does a lot of volunteer work for various community groups. She makes sure to include some social time with friends in her busy schedule. And she's tired. As many of us are, she is in the process of reevaluating her vision of what she wants life to be like for herself and her daughter. This all sounds pretty good on paper. The problem is, she is so busy keeping up with her daily commitments that despite her heartfelt desire to make some changes and deal with some issues in her life, she can't ever seem to get around to it. She needs to rest. Maybe you do, too.

3. *We fear failure.* Maybe we're a hotshot realtor able to solve other people's housing problems, but when it comes to solving problems under our own roof, we fear failure. Perhaps we feel insecure because of personal limitations. Everyone has them. None of us can do everything we want to do. That means that there will be obvious gaps in our competency and that we will sometimes fail. But that's okay. We're human beings, and human beings are not perfect.

Some personal limitations we can change. Others we can't. If you have a problem with impatience—with your children, your spouse, your friends, your colleagues—you might want to take a look at your expectations of these people and yourself. Do you want too much from them? Are you not getting enough rest, play, or exercise? Are you willing to look at this from the perspective that it's *your* problem, not theirs?

On the other hand, some personal limitations are givens. If I'm not tall enough to reach the top cupboards in my kitchen, I have two options: not put anything there at all or move often-used items to lower shelves and buy a stool so I can reach the seldom-used items I store there.

Sometimes we fear failure because we feel we lack certain skills. In this case we need to ask, Are the relevant skills crucial to my solving the problem? Can I train myself or be trained to do them? Can I limp along doing something until my skill level improves?

As you consider whether you lack the specific skills to solve a particular problem,

> "The greatest mistake you can make is to be continually fearing you will make one."
> —Elbert Hubbard
>
> "Let us be of good cheer, however, remembering that the misfortunes hardest to bear are those which never come."
> —James Russell Lowell

think about whether you personally need to develop the necessary skills or whether you can delegate the job or hire someone else to do it. For instance, do you need to learn accounting skills or could you hire the services of a good accountant at tax time?

4. *We fear criticism or rejection.* Criticism, valid or not, can hurt so much we're tempted to stop wanting something better. Sad to say, but many times those closest to us—husbands, mothers, fathers, siblings, associates, competitors—can all raise significant barriers. They either create problems or seem to want to prevent us from solving them. We have to accept who these people are. Sometimes we need to confront them, lovingly but honestly, with how their criticism is part of the problem. Sometimes we simply need to accept them for themselves, as we accept ourselves for ourselves.

5. *We build imaginary roadblocks.* Remember the enlarging machine? It takes a small incident and expands it to fill our minds. We worry and fret about possible problems that don't yet exist. This needlessly drains us of precious emotional energy we need to deal with what's at hand.

Action

Oh, would that we were all completely logical, rational beings. Yeah, sure, and that chocolate didn't have any calories. The logical thing to do

How to Respond to Criticism

Here are seven tips that will help you face your critics—at home or the office.

1. First, stop what you are doing and look directly in the eyes of your critic. Actively listen to what he or she is saying. If you are on the phone, tell the person that you are listening. Don't interrupt. Let your critic talk.
2. Try to listen in between the lines—discern what is going on behind the remarks. It could be that you are the object of someone's pent-up frustration or hormones, with nothing personal intended.
3. Realize and accept that the criticism is the other person's perspective, which he or she believes to be correct. Therefore, it doesn't do any good to accuse the critic of being oversensitive or irrational. If the criticism is exaggerated, don't get hung up trying to correct the critic on the spot.
4. Don't evade the issue or bring up another topic. Deal with it.
5. Don't make fun of the criticism, as it may be a sensitive issue from the critic's perspective. You may be perceived as sarcastic and belittling.
6. Try to remain open and find any truth in the criticism. Nobody's perfect. Usually, there is at least something valid, even if it's poppy-seed size, to the critic's words.
7. After you've listened to the criticism, ask for an opportunity to respond. Begin by restating what you heard the critic saying to make sure you understood. Then, share what you feel about the criticism and what you believe to be true. Admit what you think is correct about the criticism. Share your thoughts and feelings in a controlled manner.

once we've adjusted our attitude and considered our options is to act on the problem to solve it. On paper, it's as simple as counting to three. In real life, it might be a different story. Sometimes we need to take action—perhaps one small step at a time or perhaps a major change, even though our attitude fights us every inch of the way.

We need to realize that sometimes attitudes follow actions. When we lead with our actions—do what is right, even though we don't feel like it—sometimes miraculously our attitude will follow. At times I feel cool toward Bill because he doesn't seem to understand the demands of my two full-time jobs. This is a problem on both his part and mine. I remind myself that he really doesn't understand, and never will fully. Nor do I fully understand his life and his problems. Sometimes simply sitting close to him on the couch or giving him a hug turns the tide. I begin to remember why I married him in the first place.

I'm not suggesting we can make problems disappear by acting as if they aren't there. But we certainly won't solve problems by not doing anything about them. When we take positive action, positive attitude follows.

The attitude/action idea of solving problems is not a script for a thirty-minute television show. It's more like knitting. You start with a ball of yarn. You cast on the first row of stitches. You keep adding to the rows a stitch at a time, trying to make them as even as possible. Sometimes you make a mistake or drop a stitch. Then you go back, undo what you've done, and start again from that point. Eventually you have a sweater—or a metaphor for a way of taking action that doesn't look exactly like we're moving toward a solution. We can take the action of doing something positive daily to improve our attitude. This might be something as simple as stepping back for ten minutes when you get tense. It might be counting your blessings: I have hot water to wash my hair, a pillow for my head, heat in the house. Eventually you have a better attitude. (But only if you keep at it.) This can be an especially important strategy when we're facing difficult problems at work or home.

This small prayer has changed countless people's lives, some of them my friends. People who belong to twelve-step programs like Alcoholics Anonymous use it to remind themselves daily that there are simply some things we can't change.

> "God, give us grace to accept with serenity the things that cannot be changed, courage to change the things which should be changed, and the wisdom to distinguish the one from the other."   —Reinhold Niebuhr

Among those are our age, race, country of origin, or family of birth. And, of course, we can't change other people's minds, feelings, or actions. We need to know and accept that there are uncomfortable and unfortunate things in this life so we don't waste precious energy and get more and more frustrated trying to fix them. When we concentrate on what we *can* change, things change. It's as simple as that.

The list of what we can change is often longer than we think it is. When we know the difference, we can begin to concentrate our energies there. For instance, we might not be able to control the fact that we're having a hard time making ends meet because we've lost our job. But we can control how we choose to respond to that fact. We can't control a teenage or young adult child's choices. But we can control how we respond to those choices. Sometimes our children need to know that we love them even though we don't like what they're doing.

There are a lot of things we can control and change—our feelings, thoughts, desires, attitudes, values, state of health, education/training, and use of our time. When we're tempted to fall into the trap of being victims of circumstances outside our control, it sometimes helps to take inventory of the things we can control.

It takes practice and reflection to discern on a daily basis what's under our control and what's not. Time and again I've heard people say they'd have a problem under control if only their boss, sister, child, or spouse would do what he or she is supposed to do. They know in principle that there are things they can and can't control and that other people's behavior almost always belongs in the latter category. Yet they keep trying to control other people's behavior. We can ask other people to change. We can let them experience the consequences if they don't.

What we can't do, even with children, is make them be what we want them to be. If you find yourself repeatedly running headlong into a wall that stops you from solving problems, you might try listing

> "Do not let what you cannot do interfere with what you can do."   —John Wooden

the aspects of the problem that you can control and the ones that you can't.

If, for example, you had a small child with a behavior problem that threatened to injure himself or others—say, hitting or running out into the street—you can't, of course, let him actually hit others or run into the street. What you can do is impose the logical consequences for such behavior—time-outs, appropriated toys, confinement to the house or backyard, whatever seems appropriate. You can also talk about the consequences of behavior. And you can share what you feel when the child acts that way. What you can't do is control his urge to engage in that behavior. Once you stop trying to control the desire and start employing other strategies, the results will be different.

AN ACTION SCENARIO

Something many, if not most, dual-career women face at some time is one of those immovable-objects problems that puzzled us in science class. Here's the scenario. Your day care closes at five P.M. You are delayed at work. There is no way around it. You can't get there until five-thirty. So what you can't change in this problem is the closing time of the day-care center or the last-minute emergency at work. What do you do?

If you have a can-do attitude and consider your approach—that is, respond instead of react—you can probably come up with some simple solutions that, while not perfect, will solve the immediate problem.

1. You might be able to take some work home with you, and try to make it by five. But your car is probably low on gas; it will be rush hour. It's unlikely you'll make it in time. Besides, then you'll simply have to get back into work mode later tonight, when you don't have the time, and your project won't be on your boss's desk first thing in the morning. Discard this option.

2. Phone your backup child-pickup person, perhaps your husband or

a friend. Say that you're running late, and ask him or her to retrieve your offspring. (If you don't have a backup, lose twenty points and return to the contingency-planning section in Chapter 4.)

3. Phone your day-care center to alert them that you'll be late. Ask them to tell your child when to expect you. And volunteer to pay the late penalty. (Don't wait for them to ask. Day-care providers work for little or nothing above the minimum wage. And you're inconveniencing them.)

Each of us meets problems every day. Some are more frustrating than this one, some less. The point is, practice having a positive attitude and a flexible approach. We won't always, or even often, solve a problem for all time by taking action in a response mode. (Chances are you're going to encounter this very same problem more than once in your dual-career time as a working woman with a child in day care.) But what you will do is solve that specific problem for that specific day.

If this scenario happens frequently, you might take other action: anything from looking for a different job in a family-friendly company or finding a day-care center that's open later to approaching your boss with a request for different hours or a flexible departure time.

If at First You Don't Succeed, Keep the Goal in Sight

Every minute of every day gives us a new choice, an opportunity to do things differently and produce even better results. So why, if something isn't working in our life, do we use the same behavior over and over? Making new choices that go against past habits requires commitment and risk taking. If we are honest, we will admit that many

> "I think and think for months, for years; ninety-nine times and the conclusion is false. But the hundredth time I'm right."
> —Albert Einstein

times it's easier to blame the situation than to accept the responsibility to change.

One of my mentors gave me some very good advice about solving problems. "Get up and go on" is the way she put it. Press on when you slip up. Don't beat

> "We are the one species that is able to form a judgment about what is best for us to do—and then proceed to do the opposite." —Nathaniel Branden

yourself up. It's a waste of precious time to wallow in self-pity or to drag yourself through the mud. Everyone makes mistakes.

As women and as Family Managers, we have a lot of power and influence over how our families approach the solving of problems. If we can help them see roadblocks as building blocks, the strong, decisive individuals who emerge will fashion better communities and a better country. Obviously, this is more than a worthy endeavor for us all.

Keeping Your Balance

- Respond instead of react.
- Keep the enlarging machine unplugged.
- Avoiding pain guarantees a shallow life. Facing pain and seeking to grow from it develop character.
- Practice tenacity. Patiently work through problems.
- Approach problems realizing there is something you can do and some good will likely come from them.
- Identify your personal roadblocks.
- Accept what you cannot change.
- When necessary, change. Make new choices even if they go against old patterns.

NINE
Stay on the Cutting Edge

"The wave of the future is coming and there is no stopping it."
—Anne Morrow Lindbergh

In my mid-thirties, I dreamed of becoming CEO of my own company. In my fantasy I was surrounded by a helpful staff; I had a quaint corner office with a great view and antique cherry furniture. I wore designer suits, coordinating silk shells, and large tortoiseshell glasses (kind of a Wall Street look). I juggled appointments to fit *Money* magazine into my schedule for a cover shoot. Management guru Tom Peters stopped by regularly for coffee. In my mind, I did business in a world where banks never called in their loans but Bill Gates called for advice; no one haggled over contracts, since my clients fought to outbid each other; and the IRS didn't care if I kept records as long as my office was handsomely appointed. Alas, my fantasy business came true one day, and you guessed it—it wasn't exactly what I expected.

Many days I go to work in exercise clothes. I've conducted radio interviews wearing nothing but a towel. And when I need a break after too many hours of glaring at my computer screen, instead of going out for coffee, I change the background music from Mozart to Motown, get down on the floor, and do crunches and push-ups. It's not like this every day. Many days I am dressed in a business suit. And I do meet with editors, media personnel, and business consultants. Often I'm traveling to speak at one conference or another, appearing on television and radio, conducting brainstorming sessions via conference calls. When I need to be "suitable" for the public, I am, but when I'm in my home office, I'm just as productive in my leggings.

> "Know that it is good to work. Work with love and think of liking it when you do it."
> —Brenda Ueland

What Works There Will Work Here, Too

For the Family Manager with two careers, staying on the cutting edge in both is really not an option. If we don't, we burn out, sooner or later, in one career or the other. Often women who know what they need to do to stay on the cutting edge in their outside-the-home careers miss an opportunity when they don't apply those same techniques to their Family Manager role. For instance, an attorney who subscribes to one or more professional journals might never realize that reading up on ways to keep her family running smoothly might help both careers. But it does. Here are some things that work for me. They're all things we've learned to do in our "professional" lives. It's a simple matter of translation to our "home" lives.

1. *Develop a professional Family Manager network and use it.* Even if we don't call it networking, this is probably the one professional strategy women use most commonly. Mothers of toddlers or teenagers share stories and ideas about what works and what doesn't. In this day and age, women's traditional networks—extended family and long-term friends—often aren't in place or accessible to us. We have to work at developing a network. But that network can be invaluable for sharing information, forming mentor relationships, and discovering colleagues with similar goals and like projects. That's one point of networking.

Businesspeople also use networking to scout out new jobs or new business opportunities. Say you're looking for a computer expert. You may well ask a person you meet at a professional or social gathering if she knows anyone who provides the services you're looking for. Why not do the same if you're a Family Manager looking for a painter or a carpenter or a babysitter?

If you're looking for a new job in your field or in a related one, you may well set up informational interviews in which you make contacts that could lead to that new job. If you're a Family Manager, you could use the same strategy to find other Family Managers you work with to set up a school carpool.

As you meet women at work, at your children's school, or at the playground, take the initiative to get to know them. Exchange phone numbers. Find out what your common interests and concerns are. Ask a Family Manager whose children are older than yours how she dealt with the temper tantrums of a two-year-old or the separation anxiety of a seven-year-old. When you meet someone whose organizational ability you admire, tell her so and ask for tips.

Have a monthly lunch with working mothers in your company to talk about work/family issues. Find out how your colleagues have learned to work with inflexible bosses.

One final word on networking: it works best when it works both ways. Share your one-step brownie recipe or your fail-safe method of keeping the bathroom clean. Offer information on subjects you are expert at.

2. *Stay current with new information.* Be open to new information that can help you run your home or office more efficiently. Recently when I was reading the professional newsletter *Communication Briefings*, I was intrigued by an article on teamwork entitled "What to Start, Stop, Stick To." The article suggested that managers could help team members work better as a group and be more productive by collecting their responses to these questions: What are we not doing that we should start? What are we doing that we should stop? What are we doing that we should stick to? Although this article was written for the office, the first thing that came to my mind was to try this at home with my team members there. About that same time I was reading in a women's magazine about decluttering your kitchen counters—just keeping out the things you use every day and storing or getting rid of the extras. I decided I need to apply the same principle to my desk in my office! I'm always on the lookout for ideas in whatever I'm reading that will help me in both my careers. I know a woman who says the best management motivation tip she ever read was the fence-painting scene in *The Adventures of Tom Sawyer,* which she was reading aloud to her children.

Make time to read inspiring and useful magazine articles and books. Learning new things keeps life interesting. It's time well spent. Keep magazine articles you want to read in your car. When you need to wait for the carpool or at the dentist's office, you'll have something to do. Or listen to tapes as you drive or exercise. Keep a notebook that's expressly for jotting down new ideas you read about or hear. Consider forming a book club with women from all walks of life, all ages, all backgrounds. No doubt each of you will suggest books to read that the others would never have picked up on their own.

3. *Learn new skills.* Many professions—for example, doctors, nurses, lawyers, therapists, and others that are licensed—require people to take a certain number of continuing education units per year to keep current with developments in their fields and learn new skills. Even if you aren't in one of these professions, you probably have attended seminars or classes designed to teach you new procedures or help you make more efficient use of your time.

Sometimes you can kill two birds with one stone. I know a mother of three who's a physician specializing in family practice. When she went to a required continuing education seminar recently, her oldest was about to turn thirteen. So she chose to attend a seminar about adolescent behavior and medical and psychological health in adolescence. This was material

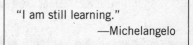

"I am still learning."
—Michelangelo

she needed for her job as a family doctor, but also for her job as a mom.

Choose educational opportunities that will allow you to learn for both careers at once. If your company sends you to a time-management seminar by all means, learn the techniques for your job, but also think about how you can apply them at home. If you're learning how to use fiscal-management software for your job, consider how you might use a simpler version of the same program at home. In fact, you might even ask the seminar teacher to recommend a home package.

Also consider taking a class or learning a new skill for your job as

How to Start a Babysitting Co-op

1. Gather a list of interested parents. Invite them to an organizational meeting and discuss the size of the group, membership requirements, election of officers, frequency of meetings, dues needed to pay for supplies, and guidelines for handling emergencies, sick children, and late pickups.

2. Establish an exchange system. Consider the ticket system—authorize an established number of tickets per child per hour. For example, charge two tickets for babysitting one child per hour, three tickets for two children, etc. Determine the average number of tickets members will use per month and distribute the same number of tickets to each member. Add the stipulation that if a member runs out of tickets, she may purchase them from another member at a predetermined rate.

3. Appoint a secretary to type and distribute rules to all members. Give her one ticket for each half hour of work.

4. Establish a system of personal record keeping for each child. Include medical and special food information, pediatrician's name and phone number, preferred hospital, insurance information, emergency contact, and a permission slip for medical treatment (check state requirements).

5. Insist that each parent write down where he/she can be reached each time a child is left.

Family Manager. This might be a course on furniture reupholstering or a seminar on financial planning for college expenses and retirement. It might be a class on cooking quickie meals, a workshop on building relationships, a brief "apprenticeship" under a master party/event planner, the use of a new day-planning system, or a seasonal hiking group for fun and exercise. Or consider taking a class with an older child or your spouse. The whole family might enjoy kayaking lessons. Or sign up for a class held while your child is taking one. One mom I know takes an exercise class while her daughter takes piano classes at a local university.

4. *Bartering is an old idea whose time has come around again.* A babysitting cooperative is probably the most common form we hear about these days. When my children were younger, some friends and I set up a babysitting cooperative. We created a board of directors and established procedures and rules about location of sitting, time availability, and rate of exchange. This was much like setting up a business plan for a new venture, and because we implemented businesslike parameters, the endeavor went smoothly. There are lots of other things you can barter. Start a toy-swapping club with other moms. Trade toys that your own kids don't mind living without for a week or two. Your kids will love getting a new set of toys every few weeks, and they'll learn some good lessons about sharing. Or follow the example of a group of Family Managers from Texas: start a dinner co-op. You cook dinner for everyone in the co-op one day a week and deliver it. In return, dinner is delivered to your door four days a week. Find four other moms who have similar family sizes, cooking abilities, and lifestyles. (If your family tries to eat low-fat, for example, you wouldn't want to be in a co-op with families who serve primarily high-fat foods.) Arrange a time to meet to talk about food preferences, food allergies, cooking days, menus, delivery times, etc. Next, purchase sealable, microwavable, dishwasher-safe container sets. Each set should include an entree container, two side dishes, and a salad bowl. Each family needs to purchase four complete sets. (For more information contact Co-op Cuisine, 2240 Morriss Road, Suite 110/189, Flower Mound, Texas 75028.)

Bartering for dreaded tasks worked for two dual-career women, Katy and Lori. Katy hates housework but loves yard work. Lori hates to get dirt under her fingernails, but gets a great deal of satisfaction from cleaning her home. So by mutual agreement, they trade services. One day a week Katy takes care of all the yard work for both homes while Lori does the housecleaning. It's a win-win proposition.

Businesses often barter their services, and it's easy to adapt some of their practices as a Family Manager:

- When trading goods or services, put the details in writing. To ensure delivery of the promised goods or services, write up an agreement, date it, and have both parties sign it.
- Hang a notice on a bulletin board at your office, church, synagogue, child's school, local library—anyplace where people can post services and skills they are willing to barter.
- Start a neighborhood trade day when services and items are swapped.
- Ask your local newspaper to begin a swap column.

To get started saving money through bartering, you first need to establish what skill or property you have to offer in a bartering deal. Your sewing, project-planning, computer, or decorating skills may be just the thing someone else needs. Then make a list of things you would just as soon have someone else do or things you'd like to learn. Then whenever you have a job to be done or need to buy an item, think first about who might be willing to barter with you.

Bartering can be a one-time arrangement or an ongoing enterprise. Offer to teach a friend a bookkeeping system in exchange for cooking lessons. Tutor a neighbor's child in English in return for an oil change. The list of possibilities is nearly endless. If you are good at organizing,

once you get the hang of bartering, you
may want to start a bartering club to help
connect dual-career women who would
like to use each other's skills or services.

> "Invention breeds invention."
> —Ralph Waldo Emerson
>
> "An investment in knowledge
> always pays the best interest."
> —Benjamin Franklin

On a large or small scale, bartering
can make a difference in your family fi-
nances by keeping more cash in your pocket. Swapping can bring previously unaffordable items into reach.

A Word on Return on Investment

American businesses have been criticized for being shortsighted, for
paying attention to only the bottom line for the next quarter. Of course
the financial bottom line will always be important in businesses and
families. Neither of them operate too well for long periods in the red.
But paying attention to only the short-term return on investment can be
disastrous for businesses and families. Lately I've been reading about other
factors corporations are taking into account when they count return on
investment. Will their investment benefit the company in the long run?
Will it attract new customers? Will it attract creative, innovative employees who will help the company grow? Are its policies socially and
ecologically responsible? Is it giving something back to the community?

I submit that as Family Managers we have to ask ourselves a similar
set of questions to stay on the cutting edge. I often hear "I don't have
the time [or energy or money] to take a class, read a book, get together
with women friends." Okay, I'm the first to admit that it's sometimes
hard to find extra time or money. But I'm also a firm believer in where
there's a will, there's a way.

When you want to try something new but find yourself resisting
the urge because of a lack of time, money, or energy, ask yourself
what you'll gain by doing it. Will you be happier or more content; have a
new skill you can use to change jobs or perhaps eventually begin

> "I do not fear computers. I fear the lack of them."
> —Isaac Asimov

your own business; or be able to make your home more beautiful, more organized, and more peaceful? Is that something you want? If your answer is yes, I say go for it. The return will be worth it.

Cutting-edge Tools for Family Managers

The same tools that have revolutionized the way most people do business in the last few years can revolutionize the way we manage our families. No single tool is a miracle cure, of course. I learned this little gem of truth via trial and error with my brand-new microwave oven. No doubt I was influenced by exaggerated advertising claims that I would suddenly become an accomplished cook who could prepare gourmet meals in ten minutes. The reality was something quite different. But now I can't imagine living without my microwave, and it has changed some food routines around our house. Bill and I periodically have cooking days. He's the head chef and I'm the sous-chef in charge of gathering the ingredients, providing the equipment, and cleaning up. We prepare soups, casseroles, stews, and other labor-intensive dishes ahead of time and freeze them. Then, with the not-a-miracle-but-it-still-helps-a-lot microwave, we can have balanced, appealing, nourishing meals ready in about ten minutes.

Another major tool for me is my computer. When I began writing, I used a computer only for typing up the text because it's a lot faster than handwriting three hundred pages! Now not only do I use my computer for writing, I also use it to organize my life. Over time, I've become dependent on my computer—in a good way. Experience has taught me that I save a lot of time managing my family's schedules, financial information, vacation plans, menus, shopping lists, and so on, using my computer.

When I sat down to actually think about all the different ways my computer helps me save time, I discovered that it comes in handy for all seven departments of Family Management. Moreover, 30 percent of women buyers in the past two years set up their computers themselves— a statistic that confirms that it's easy to do yourself. No more excuses.

Here are some ways to make your computer work for you.

HOME AND PROPERTY

Maintain a current and complete home inventory to prevent hours of rummaging and calculating in the event of a burglary, fire, or natural disaster. (Keep a current backup disk of your hard drive in a safe place off the premises.)

Keep a file for your car that includes car repairs, oil and air-filter changes, mileage records, and insurance information. This provides a quick reference in case of accidents or breakdowns.

FOOD

Have several different weekly menus on file which you can use every month or two.

Keep your recipes on file to prevent losing your grandmother's best apple pie recipe.

Cooking software gives you the choice of thousands of recipes, organizes the ones you have, allows you to consult a cooking glossary, and converts ordinary recipes into healthy or light dishes.

FAMILY AND FRIENDS

Maintain an accurate record of each family member's medical history, allergies, doctors' visits, and vaccinations to pull up in the event of a health crisis or problem. Software programs for recording your family's medical history allow you to make charts and graphs of just about anything, including day-to-day changes in your blood pressure.

Consult one of the many on-line doctors to diagnose the common cold, flu, and other easily treatable viruses or ailments. The information you quickly receive from the Internet saves wasted time at the doctor's office.

Get your kids hooked on a fun, educational game on the computer and take a couple of hours to clean, catch up on work, or read a book on a weekend morning.

Allow the computer to cut your time as your child's tutor in half. Use programs for teaching grammar, spelling, and math to supplement your tutoring and free you up for an hour. If your children use the Internet to do research, be aware of things out there you don't want them to see and monitor time closely. The best way I know of to prevent your child from cruising into dangerous areas on the information superhighway is to make sure a parent is along for the ride—or close by and checking in frequently.

Keep in touch with far-away friends and family by using e-mail. We find that with kids in two different states, e-mail saves us a lot of money. We can "talk" daily for pennies.

Keep an address book on your computer. Even if you believe that it's tacky to send holiday greeting cards or party invitations out addressed with printed labels, the computer is a convenient place to keep addresses. Unlike an address book, a computer is hard to lose, and keeping your addresses up to date is easy.

FINANCES

Install a program that allows you to conduct most banking tasks from your personal home computer. Avoid sprints to the bank.

Use financial software to balance your checkbook, create budgets, pay bills, and organize your finances. The computer can even take your transaction history and instantly turn it into a workable plan for future spending.

SPECIAL PROJECTS

Use information on the Internet to plan your family's vacation. Software allows you to research information about destinations, itineraries, lodging, suggestions for trips, accessible restaurants and ATMs, and local weather. Order your plane tickets through the Internet as well.

Create a file for all addresses for Christmas and Hanukkah cards. Use software to create your own greeting cards, picture books, calendars, or certificates of merit. The kids can go for hours on this one.

TIME AND SCHEDULING

Shop on-line for clothes, household appliances, and just about anything else you can imagine. Most nationally recognized merchants have on-line sites, and thousands more small stores are opening them daily.

Use personal-information-manager software to check for conflicts in your family's schedule. Input all the information and watch it organize and monitor the events.

Keep grocery and household shopping lists on file and print one out before you go shopping.

Five Timesaving Computer Tips

- E-mail and fax clients and contacts instead of sending letters or calling on the telephone.
- If you have work to be done on the computer, suggest to your boss that you will do it at home.
- Do research on the Internet instead of going to a public library.
- Read your favorite magazine on-line instead of going out and buying it.
- Keep a log of how many fat grams and calories you eat and how long you exercise.

PERSONAL

The computer can save hours at work and, as a result, give you more
time for other tasks. Use the time for your own personal growth,
relaxation, or rest.

Voice Mail

In the past few years, I've heard and made my own share of disparaging
remarks or jokes about voice-mail jail. Yes, it's frustrating to phone for
reservations or to get a problem solved and hear that mechanical voice
tell you to press 1 if this, but 2 if that, 3 on the other hand, 4 for none
of the above, and 5 if it's after four in Holland. If what you want isn't
one of the options, well, good luck. On the other hand, voice mail can
be a lifesaver. We have a system that allows for multiple boxes on one
telephone number. People wanting to leave messages for Bill or me or
the boys can do so by pressing 1, 2, 3. It's that simple. We can also leave
messages for each other.

Other tools that we regularly use in business that can make our
Family Management jobs easier include cell phones and pagers.

Work Your Job, Don't Let It Work You

When many of the two-career women I know talk about making
changes in their lives to make them more rewarding or reasonable, they
talk about changes they can make at home. They want ideas for meal
planning or scheduling or routines that make their home run better.
Often these same women don't think that they have any control over or
options for making their outside careers more manageable, which would
also help make their lives more rewarding or reasonable (sometimes pro-
foundly!). Our jobs often seem like all-or-nothing propositions: spend
forty, sixty, or more hours a week commuting and doing a job the way
we've always done it—or quit.

In fact, there are almost always other options. If they truly don't exist for you in the job you're now in, one way to stay on the cutting edge is to think about what you'd need to do to take advantage of other options like job sharing, working part time, working flextime, or starting your own at-home business. This might be something as dramatic as taking out an education loan (no, they're not just for kids) so you can learn new skills for a new profession. Or it might mean advertising in professional journals and networking to find someone to share a job with you. Here's how one woman I know took advantage of the fact that her job was largely an independent one and moved herself from her downtown office to her home office through a series of well-considered steps.

TELECOMMUTING

Working from home, either independently or telecommuting, is becoming more popular and more doable for many women. Perhaps it is for you, too. For Michelle, it was a job-, time-, and money-saver.

Michelle worked as an editor at a large publishing company for nine years. She took three months off when her daughter was born, then went back to work part time, twenty-five hours a week. Five years later she had a problem. Her daughter was now kindergarten age. Her day-care provider took only preschoolers and the school didn't have on-site after-school care.

Michelle studied her options: she could quit her job, but her family needed the income. She could look into off-site after-school day care, but transportation was a problem. She didn't have extended family close by to help out, so that wasn't an option. Then she thought of investigating the possibility of working at home. She decided to create a tele-commuting plan and convince her boss to say yes. After a short period of negotiations, he agreed.

She shared her strategy with me in the hopes that it would help other women who want to do the same. If you wonder whether tele-commuting or working part time from home is a viable alternative for you, go over the following questions with ruthless honesty.

IS WORKING AT HOME AN OPTION FOR YOU?

1. Are you self-directed and do you work well independently? In past evaluations, how has your employer rated you on time management and productivity? Good scores are positive evidence you can use to prove to your employer (or yourself) that you can work at home.

2. Realistically, can your job be done away from a corporate office environment? Does it require uninterrupted concentration? Do you need a lot of space and special equipment? Can your job be done using a computer, fax, modem, e-mail, pager, and/or voice mail? Will the company provide those? If not, can you cover the costs?

3. Would a compressed work week—three twelve-hour days or four ten-hour days—work as well or better than your current system?

4. How will your boss supervise you? How often will you need to attend meetings at the office? Can he or she evaluate your work if you work at home?

5. What benefits can you sell to your employer? Fewer days off from work (a sick child no longer means missed hours)? Increased flexibility to meet client and corporate needs—special projects can be done after regular work hours? Reduced need for office and parking? Increased employee satisfaction? Will the company save money if you reduce your hours? The key to negotiating the job schedule you want is to make your employer see that he or she will gain from the arrangement as well.

6. If you lose some or all of your benefits, can you afford to cover them yourself?

After answering these questions, if you see that telecommuting or working from home might work, research child-care options. Find short-term child care for your children when you are away from home. Also, have a child-care plan for the summer. Make sure your employer knows that you will not care for your children on company time.

Then write a formal proposal stating your request to work from home. Include the date you want to start. Summarize why you believe

Tips for Successfully
Working at Home with a Toddler

I first started working part time from an at-home office when my youngest son was two. It took some adjustment. I learned some good work habits that have served me well in many different ways over the years.

- Be extremely disciplined with time. Learn to use naptime or time when your child is at preschool to do the high-concentration jobs.
- Think of projects in their component parts. If you don't have time to finish a whole thing, use the time to finish parts of it.
- Set up a "home office" for your child with art supplies, paper, pencils, tape, and an old briefcase. One of my toddler's favorite games became "working," and he became so engrossed in it that I got extra chunks of time to work in.
- Trade with other mothers from preschool or the neighborhood for child care.
- Screen all phone calls with an answering machine or voice mail while your child is in preschool or day care. That way you protect your high-focus time. And when you call back, you won't be tempted to talk as long, since your child will need your attention.
- Set up rules about being quiet "when Mommy is on the phone." Do something fun together as a reward for following the rules.

your job is appropriate for telecommuting and describe your proposed daily routine. Suggest a specific length of time for a trial period. Remember that your boss may need approval from those above him or her, especially if your company has never had an employee work from home. A well-written proposal will get him or her on your side.

Even if you don't have a toddler, most of these tips will help. School-age children present another set of challenges. I have been known to proofread a manuscript and watch a baseball game at the same time. I've also learned that working at home provides a flexibility that makes my life simpler in a lot of ways. I can do errands and shopping during the day or work after my kids are asleep. I still focus on component parts while keeping the big picture in mind.

I think there are benefits for kids of working mothers as well, whether those moms have an office at home or away from home. I know one freelance editor whose teenage daughter occasionally helps her with administrative chores. Her daughter earns a bit of money and learns skills that will benefit her in later life, and she gets to spend time with her mom. My hunch is that children of two-career moms learn more independent living skills sooner because two-career moms need help with cooking, cleaning, running errands, and planning ahead for everything from being able to attend soccer games to making and keeping doctors' and dentists' appointments. Plus, by working wisely we're modeling that same behavior for our children.

Staying on the Cutting Edge
Can Prevent That Chopped-up Feeling

Whether you're basically satisfied with both your careers or not, staying on the cutting edge helps. It's really a simple matter of using the tools, skills, and resources from your "outside" career in your Family Management career and vice versa. Integrating these areas of your life creates an added benefit: your life is no longer chopped up. There's no need to segregate information gathering; everything you learn helps in both arenas. As a dual-career woman, you no longer have to maintain two separate lives; your successes in one will inevitably spill over into the other. Every effort you make is doubled through no extra exercise.

I have to say, despite never having achieved the fantasy life I described at the beginning of the chapter, I'm happy with the way things turned out. I may not have cherry furniture, but I do have (most of the time) a contented, functioning family and steady income from a job I enjoy and am challenged by. That's where your real success as a dual-career woman is measured, anyway: in the faces of the people you love, and in the sigh of satisfaction you breathe when you see your plans working for you, not against you. And you know something? I never looked good in tortoiseshell glasses anyway.

Keeping Your Balance

- For the Family Manager with two careers, staying on the cutting edge in both is essential.
- Networking works best when it works both ways. Share your expertise.
- Bartering can make a difference in your family finances by keeping more cash in your pocket. Swapping can bring previously unaffordable items into reach.
- The same tools that have revolutionized the way most people do business—such as computers—can revolutionize the way we manage our families.
- Work your job, don't let it work you. There are almost always other options open to you.
- You no longer have to maintain two separate lives; your successes in one will inevitably spill over into the other.

TEN
One Life:
Live It in Balance

"The cost of success will be too high if you choose not to lead a balanced life."
—Linda Stryker

No matter how many careers we have, we have only one life. No matter how many aspirations and responsibilities we have, we have only one body—one brain, one set of hands, one heart, one soul—to use to fulfill them. If I had a dollar, or even a nickel, for every time I read an article or a book about taking care of myself, told myself to take care of myself, or was told by others to take care of myself, I would be quite literally richer than Croesus, no matter how much money he had.

When I was younger, I took this advice with a grain of salt. After all, I was strong, smart, and superambitious—immortal, in my mind. As I got older, though, reality began to drain away my naiveté. The law of gravity took effect and everything on my body started sagging toward the ground; my energy waned; my mind and emotions felt foggy. It wasn't long before all these symptoms added up to one conclusion: I needed to start taking regular, thoughtful care of myself—for survival's sake. And as if by magic, as long as I keep taking care of myself, I'm actually in better shape, with more energy, than I was ten or even twenty years ago.

Ecologically speaking, when a species can't find ways to adapt and survive, it disappears. When one species disappears, it sets off a chain reaction up and down the food chain. Here's a dictionary definition of ecology: the science of relationships between organisms and

> "Where we stand is not as important as the direction in which we are moving."
> —Oliver Wendell Holmes, Jr.

their environments. Every organism in nature is dependent in some way—often in ways we don't even understand the full implications of—on the survival skills of another. In recent years, we've become more aware as a society about what impact we're having on our environment by living the way we do. From community recycling projects to corporate and government projects to reclaim polluted waters or clean up landfills, we've come a long way. And we have a long way to go. Ecology is, in fact, an ongoing process, on a global level and on a personal level.

As with a species, if I burn out and take myself out of action, I not only cease living myself, but the people who depend on me are equally at a loss. So are the people who depend on them. Ecology is the science of interdependence—and it's all about balance.

When I think about two careers and one life, as you know by now, I think a lot about balance. In this book I've talked quite a bit about balancing the various aspects of our lives as it relates to managing two careers. In fact, some of us, at various times depending on our situations, have even more than two careers to balance. I think of a woman who's going to school plus managing a family plus working a job. Or I think of the many middle-aged members of the so-called sandwich generation who need to put increasing time and energy into helping their parents and/or in-laws out financially, emotionally, physically, in addition to managing their own families and careers. The word *survival* takes on new meaning.

In this chapter, I want to talk about a different kind of balance. I call it *personal ecology*. It concerns balancing our one and only life so that we can be there for the others in our lives, as well as for ourselves. It's about taking care to see that the different aspects of our system—the physical, emotional, mental, and spiritual—are in balance with one another. We are then capable of meeting the demands of our lives with the energy they require.

Making Our Way to the Middle

Personal ecology has everything to do with interdependence *within* ourselves. If we are not internally balanced, then it's almost impossible for us to maintain a stable ecology in our environment—work, home, community, the world.

We find our personal ecological balance by starting where we are. Some of us may be too rigid, some too lax. Some of us may work too hard and play not at all. Some of us may need to work harder. Sometimes personal ecology means following the rules we're given. Sometimes it means having the fortitude to let ourselves relax and take a vacation, or toss out old rules and replace them with new ones.

A good friend of mine I'll call Linda works too hard, in my judgment and hers. She's admitted several times that that's the case, but something finally clicked in a conversation she had with her daughter, Sarah, and her daughter's friend, Tom. At the time, seventeen-year-old Sarah was a high school senior, the class president, and an honor student who was waiting to hear from the nine colleges she'd applied to. She was working to raise money for the prom and several other senior-class causes, and was taking two advanced placement classes.

"She is a wonderful kid," Linda told me. "But she's totally stressed out. She keeps trying to do more and more and more. The other night she had Tom over for dinner, and the whole time she was worrying. When I told her that she needed to do less and relax more, Tom started laughing. I know him pretty well, so I asked him why he thought that was funny. He told me I didn't sound like a mom.

> "Going beyond is as bad as falling short."
> —Chinese folk wisdom

Moms should tell kids to do better, do more. I looked him in the eye and said, in all good humor, that if I was his mom I might not be giving the same advice, since every kid is different."

The real lesson came for Linda as she thought about what she said that night. "I realized it was a classic case of do as I say, not as I do," she told me. True, sometimes moms need to urge their kids on. Tom's problem was underachievement, but Linda's—and thus Sarah's—was overachievement. As a mom Linda had always been careful about saying the right things regarding balance. What she hadn't been careful about was following her own advice. "I keep coming back to that dinner," Linda said to me again recently. "I need to encourage Sarah to find balance in her life by finding my own between work and rest, doing and being. I need more fun in my life."

Many of us need to make similar analyses. Many of us need to do less or do things differently. Many of us need to remind ourselves what we're teaching our kids when our words don't match our actions.

There are a number of areas in which we would do well to evaluate how strong our sense of balance is. Do you recognize yourself in Linda's story? Or in any of the following?

Contemplating/Taking Action. A woman I'll call Ann tends to deliberate, to consider all the possible options before doing something like rearranging the living-room furniture. She sits and stares at it night after night, wondering what she can do, wishing she could come up with a better arrangement. Instead of moving even an end table, she mulls over each possibility. But she never tries any of them. Ann spends all of her energy contemplating and imagining. Consequently the furniture never gets moved, and Ann gets more frustrated.

Others/Self. I have another friend I'll call Helen who is the ultimate helper. She's the kind of person who, when we

> We all need to bring our lives into ecological balance, to find the middle ground.

moved to a new house, came over and according to my directions un-
packed all of my kitchen stuff and put it away. When I had a baby, she
cleaned my bathrooms before I came home from the hospital. (Now
that's a real friend.) Not only did Helen do things like this for me, she
did them for other friends as well. It gave her real joy to serve others.
But when any of us offered to do something for Helen, she wouldn't let
us. So she gave and gave and gave to others. Then one day she had a ner-
vous breakdown. She gave so much to others, yet never received, from
others or herself, that she became unbalanced.

In each of these scenarios, what are some possible steps to rebal-
ance? Ann could get up and start pushing chairs around just to see what
might happen. Even an unsatisfactory new arrangement could spark
some ideas for one that would work. The key is, she needs to combine
ideas with action to make any progress at all.

Helen could have decided to accept help when she needed it. She
could have decided to put aside her discomfort with being in need and
discovered the joy of receiving.

Here are some more areas where it's a good idea to find the middle
ground. I've set them up as continuums, so 10 on either side is way
off balance. The middle ground is zero, the bull's eye, the balance we
strive for.

Read this section slowly. Take time to contemplate (but if you're an
Ann, not too much time). Circle your current spot on each one. Then
beneath each one, jot down three or four specific ways you might move
toward the middle.

Productivity																				Recreation
10	9	8	7	6	5	4	3	2	1	0	1	2	3	4	5	6	7	8	9	10

If you get all of your Hit List items crossed off every day, congratulations. But consider whether you're working too hard, trying to do too much. Most people tend to put more than they can do on any given day's list. Maybe you need to put Playing front and center, near the top of yours.

On the other hand, if you cross everything off most days, but still nearly always feel frustrated and unsatisfied because there's a lot that's left undone, maybe you need to add more items to your list and figure out a way to do them.

Confidence is good. Humility is good—like everything else here—in moderation. How do people in your life respond to you? Sometimes when we think we're exuding confidence, we're exuding arrogance instead. Sometimes instead of our confidence instilling inspiration in others, it instills fear. We look more like a formidable authority figure than a confident leader.

A little genuine humility goes a long way. It's good to recognize our

Confidence																				Humility
10	9	8	7	6	5	4	3	2	1	0	1	2	3	4	5	6	7	8	9	10

Human Element																				Bottom Line
10	9	8	7	6	5	4	3	2	1	0	1	2	3	4	5	6	7	8	9	10

own shortcomings and to give others credit for shared effort. But beware of false modesty.

I think we could safely assume that most of us would say that people are more important than things or money. Yet sometimes the way we treat money or things is reflective of how we treat ourselves or others. Are you too careful with money and resources? Or are you careless? Do you attach too much importance to what others think of you and your children (another way of being too focused on the bottom line)? Do you give up things like exercise and fun with friends and family to work more? Do you find yourself flying off the handle when a child accidentally breaks a glass?

Are you willing to be merciful with yourself and others when you or they make mistakes? To cut yourself some slack? On the other hand, do you thoughtlessly forgive all mistakes and refuse to judge any action—your own or others'?

Judgment																				Grace
10	9	8	7	6	5	4	3	2	1	0	1	2	3	4	5	6	7	8	9	10

Leading																				Following
10	9	8	7	6	5	4	3	2	1	0	1	2	3	4	5	6	7	8	9	10

Are you willing to take a stand, to step out and lead your family according to the priorities you've set? Are you willing to lead yourself in that direction by learning new skills, reading, and doing the things you need to do to be in the tip-top physical and mental shape a leader needs to be in? Are you leading your family and yourself with a carrot or a cattle prod? Are you willing to follow the lead of others in getting things done? If your husband suggested that the two of you get into better shape by working out half an hour a day together, what would your response be?

This one is pretty obvious. Talking all the time, including to ourselves, is not a good thing. But then again, neither is saying nothing. Yes, we need to listen to others and we need to speak up and say what we think, need, believe, and want as clearly as possible in a variety of situations every day. The best way I know to get clear on what it is we need and want—especially when we're talking intangibles, like living in balance for ourselves and our families—is to listen to ourselves. And sometimes it's our bodies we don't listen to. Are you eating when you're

Speaking																				Listening
10	9	8	7	6	5	4	3	2	1	0	1	2	3	4	5	6	7	8	9	10

"I don't want to get to the end of my life and find that I lived just the length of it. I want to have lived the width of it as well." —Diane Ackerman

"Behind every working woman is an enormous pile of unwashed laundry." —Barbara Dale

"All things are difficult before they are easy." —John Norley

hungry? Sleeping when you're tired? Getting exercise to prevent that sluggish feeling?

By now you've gotten the picture. Some other areas you may want to evaluate yourself in are Structure/Spontaneity, Duty/Freedom, Society/Solitude, and Head-work/Hand-work.

It's Your Life

Of course, our lives are our lives; we each only have one. But how we spend our days affects everyone else's: our children, our spouses, our extended family and friends, our larger community. We all have responsibilities to other people. As we achieve personal balance we have more energy to reach out and achieve balance with the others in our lives. To me, personal ecology means taking care of myself physically, mentally, emotionally, and spiritually.

When is the last time you looked at magazine covers in the supermarket? I can't get through a checkout line without seeing banner headlines that promise me an exercise program I can do in minutes a day to get back the body I had when I was twenty-five. Or a diet that will allow me to lose ten pounds in two weeks. Or a technique for personal meditation that will put me in touch with my spiritual power in ten minutes. Or a baker's dozen of ideas to improve my mind in half an hour. Or an article that promises to make me happy all the time. We all know it isn't that easy.

Take it from a fellow struggler. What is easy is to neglect the care of ourselves. After all, our bodies, our minds, our spiritual and emotional sides aren't screaming at us like the people and projects that demand our attention. But this is one time when the squeaky wheel isn't the one that should get the grease. In fact, if it seems to you like your family, your colleagues, and your spouse are overwhelming you with requests and you feel on the verge of an eruption, you are probably in danger of crashing and burning. We really don't have much choice. If we don't take care of ourselves in the long run we won't be around to take care of business, family, or anything else.

Seven Principles for Achieving Balance

1. *Know what drains and replenishes you emotionally, and know how to find the middle ground between the two.* When we have emotional energy, when we are emotionally resilient, we can confront our problems with a sense of hope and power. When our emotional reserves are depleted, we are seriously weakened, lacking in perspective. Our strength is sapped, our resolve is paralyzed, and we become even more emotionally vulnerable, which opens the door for more depletion of emotional energy.

No matter how much emotional energy we start with at the beginning of the day, and no matter how fast or slowly we are giving it and replenishing it through interchange with our environment (that is, people, tasks, and situations) one thing is certain and universal: our emotional energy is finite; it is limited. When our reserves are depleted, we need to replenish them. If we continue to make "withdrawals," we will become overdrawn. And just like at the bank, it costs us.

We must understand what our limits are and what kinds of things deplete or recharge us. This brings us to the importance of knowing ourselves. This may sound selfish, but it isn't. Because to the extent that we know and understand who we are as human beings, to that same extent we will be able to maintain balance and serve others, carrying out our myriad responsibilities in our two careers.

> "When one is a stranger to oneself then one is estranged from others too. If one is out of touch with oneself, then one cannot touch others."
> —Anne Morrow Lindbergh

Five Ways to Fill Your Emotional Tank

1. Spend some time with a friend who makes you laugh.
2. Make a list of everything for which you are thankful.
3. Open your windows and let as much light as possible come into your home and office. If you don't have a nice view, put a pretty window box full of colorful flowers outside your window or on the window sill.
4. Display things around your home or work environment that bring fond memories to mind.
5. Whether at home or at work, focus on positive things at mealtime. The brain creates body chemicals that counteract effective digestion when we worry, fret, argue, or process negative thoughts.

Your environment can be emotionally depleting if you let things get really messy. If your work chair isn't comfortable or the lighting is bad, you feel more drained at the end of a workday than you would otherwise. An unresolved quarrel with a friend is an obvious emotional drain. A minor physical problem like a bum knee can also drain you emotionally. Debt or any other chronic family worry also depletes us emotionally. We need to take time to take care of these things. We also need to take steps to replenish ourselves so we have the energy to keep tackling the things that deplete us.

We all know what depletes us. The regular demands of our schedules—working, making sure our children are where they need to be, helping solve their emotional problems—all serve to "disempower" us every day.

Even when we understand the principle, I think we're likely to fall into two traps. One is that we simply don't do it. We don't take time to fill ourselves up. The other trap is even more dangerous and requires even more self-knowledge and honesty and effort to avoid on our part. We know we're not exempt from having our reserves depleted. But instead of doing what we know we should, we try mental tricks instead. They go something like this: *What I'm doing is such good work, is so helpful to others, is so important to the people in my life that I will just keep on doing it—at any cost.*

> No one is exempt from the debit/credit law of emotional energy, ever.

This sounds almost admirable, doesn't it? But it's deceptive. The truth is—and our bodies prove this regularly—we all need quiet and solitude. No one can expend energy indefinitely (as Helen proved above). We need to relax, sleep in, take a nap, unplug the phone, enjoy

---

Working More. Enjoying Life Less?

Pick one item from this list to do for yourself each week. Vary your choices according to your mood. Add your own ideas to the list.

- Pick up a box lunch at a favorite tea room and take yourself on a picnic at a beautiful place.
- Spend a few extra dollars to get your hair cut by a real hair designer.
- Get your nails done, even if it's not a special occasion.
- Buy a book that teaches you to do something that pleases you like making flower arrangements.
- Spend the night at a bed and breakfast—by yourself. Take your favorite magazines and a good book.
- Treat yourself to a recording of your favorite music.
- Sign up for lessons to learn something you've always wanted to do—tap dancing, ballet, painting, piano.
- Give yourself the gift of hiring someone to clean your house.
- Buy yourself a bouquet of flowers. Put them on your desk.
- Enjoy a massage from a professional masseuse.
- Give yourself a facial, or get a professional facial.
- Make an appointment with a makeup consultant.
- Take yourself to a museum.
- Write down your ten most favorite fun things to do, along with the last time you did them. Do them, starting with the one you did longest ago.

"Friendship with oneself is all-important, because without it one cannot be a friend with anyone else in the world."
—Eleanor Roosevelt

"Life is partly what we make it and partly what it is made by the friends we choose."
—Chinese proverb

a walk. In my own busy, crazy life, when I feel a depletion crisis coming on, I pack up a good book and a few snacks and go out to a friend's sailboat. It's in a slip at the marina. But there's just something about simply sitting on a boat that's relaxing. There's no phone, no TV, nothing but waves lapping, gentle wind blowing, and birds flying overhead.

Or maybe you find an aerobics exercise class, where dancing and laughing with a lot of others is the way to replenishing. Sometimes it helps just to fix yourself something beautiful and healthy to eat, put your favorite music on, and sit down to enjoy your own company. Or buy yourself some fancy soap or bath salts and luxuriate in a warm tub.

2. *Balance the different types of people you include in your life.* There are three kinds of people in our lives: those who refresh us, those who drain us, and those who are neutral. Again, balance is important. This is not about dumping all the people from our lives who drain us. "Doing nothing for others is the undoing of one's self," said Horace Mann. Giving to others helps us keep balanced. As we nourish others, we are nourished ourselves. The trick is to not have more drainers than replenishers in your life.

The other trick is to be careful about how we choose to spend time with the different types of people. If you have a drainer among your family or friends, you might choose to do something active with her rather than going out to a restaurant where you spend lots of money to simply listen to her complain about how terrible her life is or ask you for advice she's probably not going to follow anyway. If you're walking on the beach while she's talking, at least you're getting exercise. Spend a larger portion of time with those who refresh you, listen to you, give back to you. Invest your time in friendships that are two-way.

Ten Tips for Getting Fit

1. Look at your schedule. Notice where you have a blank—even for just thirty minutes. Could you fit a ten-minute walk into that slot?

2. Make appointments to exercise. Write them on your daily planner. When you wake up in the morning and think through your day, reaffirm the time you will exercise.

3. If child care is part of your problem in scheduling time for exercise, seek the help of your husband, a neighbor, or a friend. Or trade off with another mom who is trying to find time to exercise.

4. Set realistic goals, for example, walking five more minutes every day or losing one pound of fat a month. Don't expect to lose thirty pounds in two weeks.

5. For optimal physical fitness, you'll want to work up to performing regular cardiovascular exercise like walking or bicycling three to five times per week for twenty to sixty minutes. Whatever exercise you do is beneficial, so don't worry if you can't reach this frequency at first.

6. Identify potential excuses for skipping exercise. Write these down. Brainstorm ways you can work around them. For example, how can you fit exercise into the lunch hour? Could you bring lunch from home, go for a walk, and eat at your desk, or go for a walk and stop by a deli for a salad with low-fat dressing on the way back?

7. Set out your exercise clothes. Put your exercise bag by the front door or your clothes out on the dresser the night before your "appointment." Put them on when you first wake up if you intend to exercise early, or first thing when you change from work clothes if you intend to exercise at the end of the day.

8. Make plans to exercise with a friend. This will motivate you because you will want to see your friend. Also, you will be less likely to cancel because you won't want to let your friend down.

9. Set up a reward system for yourself. Promise yourself that if you exercise for a given number of days, you will give yourself something special.

10. Keep a log of the times you've exercised. This visual reminder of your accomplishments will make you feel good about already having exercised so many times. It will also motivate you to continue.

"The happiest and most fulfilled women are those who listen to themselves."
—Maxine Ballen

"A rest-less work style produces a restless person."
—Gordon MacDonald

3. *Take care of your body.* It will be much more likely to be there when you need it. When we don't take care of ourselves physically, we feel consistently tired and overwhelmed. No matter what situation we are in, we can take at least some steps to reverse what is many times self-induced bodily deterioration. "Healing is a matter of time," wrote Hippocrates, "but it is sometimes also a matter of opportunity." If I am under-rested, overweight, and under-exercised, it is my job to change. It's a choice. Changing unhealthy habits often requires changing lifestyles. And if you are trying to change yourself, it helps to surround yourself with people who will support the changes rather than undermine them.

Only you can know your own body and how much rest you need. Some women can't function without seven or eight hours of sleep. Some do fine on five or six. The amount of sleep we need can have to do with how soundly we sleep, how hard we are working, and what other ways we find to rest between sleep periods. Diet and exercise also directly affect both quantity and quality of sleep. Instead of worrying about whether the amount you sleep is right, ask yourself what percentage of the time you feel adequately rested. Studies have shown that doing daily aerobic exercise can decrease the amount of sleep people require. Exercise provides some of the benefits of sleep in that it helps to release tension, thereby producing a feeling of relaxation and well-being. It also tends to produce deeper and less fitful sleep. We must all be students of our bodies and work in harmony with them. Also, it's important to remember that illness, heavy workloads, sadness, and stress can increase the amount of sleep your body needs.

4. *Take time to play.* According to a Harris Survey, the amount of leisure time enjoyed by the average American has decreased 37 percent since 1973. Over the same period, the average workweek, including commuting, has jumped from under forty-one hours to nearly forty-seven hours.

In a lifetime, the average American will . . .

Spend six months sitting at traffic lights waiting for them to change.
Spend one year searching through desk clutter looking for misplaced objects.
Spend eight months opening junk mail.
Spend two years trying to call people who aren't in or whose line is busy.
Spend five years waiting in lines.
Spend three years in meetings.
Learn how to operate twenty thousand different things, from drink machines to can openers to digital radio controls.
Be interrupted seventy-three times every day.
Receive six hundred advertising messages every day (television, newspapers, magazines, radio, billboards).
Watch seventeen hundred hours of television every year.
Open six hundred pieces of mail every year.
(From *Margin* by Dr. Richard A. Swenson, NavPress, 1992, p. 150)

If we do all that, surely we have time to have fun. The point is, we need to balance our heavy issues with lighter ones. We need to have fun. We all need personal time, time with family, fun with friends. Schedule free time as you would any essential unbreakable appointment. Make a list of fun things you like to do in various time categories, so when you see thirty free minutes, you won't just sit there frustrated because you don't know what to do. Keep a copy of your fun-things list at your office and at home. Some of us are so used to work that we don't know what to do with leisure time, so we usually end up either in front of the TV or shopping. TV commercials are geared to make us want

"I still find each day too short for all the thoughts I want to think, all the walks I want to take, all the books I want to read, and all the friends I want to see. The longer I live the more my mind dwells upon the beauty and the wonder of the world."   —John Burroughs

"A house is no home unless it contains food and fire for the mind as well as for the body."
—Margaret Fuller

more. When we shop as a substitute for fun we tend to buy things we don't need; then we have to work more to pay for them. The actual time spent in front of the TV is often not restful and refreshing.

5. *Be a lifelong learner.* If you're feeling like an old dog, teach yourself some new tricks. Stimulating your mind with new information—classes, books, apprenticeships—keeps it lively. Doing the opposite—thinking about the same things all the time, allowing your mind to go stale and empty of ideas—means you'll become boring and predictable, and so will your life.

When my kids were young, I wondered if I would ever have time for anything besides measuring fabric softener and playing space patrol. Then one night, while moving endless loads of clothes from the washer to the dryer, I made the decision to grab moments, any time I could, to read, study, and learn new things. If I wanted to learn new things, I realized I couldn't hold on to my excuse: "I don't have time to learn something new. I'm too busy meeting everyone else's needs." If I really wanted to pursue a personal endeavor, I could choose to do it. Besides, when I do learn new things and meet my own needs for intellectual stimulation, I come back to meeting other people's needs refreshed and often with new ideas, which is another way of getting back into balance. I also found myself pursuing some things I thought I would like but didn't. I started some classes and didn't finish them, or finished them without a sense of satisfaction. But if I hadn't explored those things, I wouldn't have discovered others, including knowing a whole lot more about what I do and think.

Does your home contain food and fire for your mind as well as your body? Do you feed your mind with good, nourishing food, or are you running on a diet of mental fast food that fills your mind up temporarily but doesn't really provide the nourishment you need to keep growing? What kinds of books and magazines are you reading? What programs do you watch on television? What new films do you go see and what videos do you rent? What new subjects and interests are you pursuing?

6. *Develop your spiritual side.* Everyone has one. Deep down we all know we are more than the body we inhabit. Our souls need attention, too, although that's not always easily apparent.

> "To keep a lamp burning we have to keep putting oil in it."
> —Mother Teresa
>
> "I have been driven to my knees many times by the overwhelming conviction that I had nowhere else to go. My own wisdom and that of all those about me seemed insufficient for that day."
> —Abraham Lincoln
>
> "Life develops from within."
> —Elizabeth Barrett Browning

We have friends who fell in love with a seventy-five-year-old house with large rooms, high ceilings, and lovely moldings. The house needed a lot of work—rewiring, new plumbing, walls moved, new kitchen appliances and bathroom fixtures—but they felt confident they could turn it into a showplace. Unfortunately, when they started to work on the house they found it was held together with paint. The entire infrastructure was decayed. What had looked so good on the outside was rotten to the core with termite damage. The contractor told my friends they were lucky that they hadn't moved into the house before starting to remodel because it was unsafe for habitation. Ceilings and floors were on the verge of collapse.

After hearing their story, I thought about how true that is for us as well if we have neglected our infrastructure—the needs of our heart, the nurturing of our spirit, the clarification of our thoughts—maybe even to the point of collapse.

There's no doubt in my mind that if I couldn't draw on God's strength and wisdom daily, I'd collapse. I simply don't have all that it takes to run my life and two careers by myself.

Keep On Growing Guidelines

Over the years, I've come up with some guidelines for being a lifelong learner. If they speak to you, I suggest you choose a few and act on them. Remember, five minutes a day spent growing intellectually may not seem like much, but that adds up to over thirty hours a year of personal "class time."

- When you find an author who stimulates you, try to read everything he or she has written.
- Set aside time to talk with your husband about politics, books, current events, etc.—not the kids, the roof, or the dog.
- Buy a good dictionary, keep it close at hand, and use it. Try to learn one new vocabulary word each week.
- Write facts you want to remember or interesting quotes in a notebook or on index cards. Categorize and file them for future reference.
- Check out "how-to" videos from the library on a subject you've always wanted to know more about.
- Start a book club in your office. Invite coworkers to read the same book, then get together once a month to discuss what you read.
- Always keep at least one good book going. If you read one book each month, you're in the company of the top one percent of the intellectuals in America.
- Attend a lecture with a friend who stimulates you. Talk about what you learned.
- Create an environment conducive to learning. Surround yourself with good books, play stimulating music, keep your desk stocked with study supplies, and turn off the TV.
- Don't be afraid to go back to school. You'll be surprised at how much you remember. I was shocked to make a decent score on the GRE at age thirty-seven.
- Fill your life with new experiences. This year I'm studying French, trying to conquer a new computer program, and learning more about health and nutrition.
- Start a list of things you're interested in. It's great to have this list when you're feeling bored. It's hard to think of new things when life seems uninteresting.
- Make a commitment to never stop learning.

7. *Remember, life is not a still life.* It's not a snapshot. Life is motion, and aren't we glad? There's an old saying about the weather in Texas: If you don't like it, just wait a minute and it will change. We might not like all the changes, but we can be ready for them by keeping ourselves balanced—living as calmly and steadily and deliberately as possible. And although there are things we can't change, when we're rested and refreshed and up to speed in body, mind, and spirit, we can come up with creative ways to keep in the middle lane.

> "When we do the best we can, we never know what miracles await."   —Helen Keller
>
> "You don't get to choose how you're going to die or when. You can only decide how you're going to live. Now."
>
> —Joan Baez

Executive Neglect vs. Neglecting the Executive

There's a concept in business called executive neglect, which sounds negative at first but is really a positive thing. What it means is that executives need to learn to neglect certain things so they can focus on others. A corollary is that they put the right people and systems in place so the job can get done, and then they don't second-guess those people. Executives should spend their time focusing on their vision or mission to keep the company on the cutting edge. As Family Managers, we can use this concept of executive neglect.

What we can't do is neglect the executive. If we don't take care of ourselves—the one body, one brain, one set of hands, one heart, one soul we have—we can't take care of our business, wherever and whatever it is.

Keeping Your Balance

- No matter how many careers we have, we have only one life.
- If I burn out and take myself out of action, I not only cease living myself, but the people who depend on me are equally at a loss.
- If we maintain balance—heed our personal ecology—we can then meet the demands of our lives, with the energy they require.
- Are you leading yourself or your family with a carrot or a cattle prod?
- The best way to get clear on what we need and want is to listen to ourselves, bodies included.
- Balance the types of people you include in your life.
- If you're feeling like an old dog, teach yourself some new tricks.
- Practice executive neglect, but don't neglect the executive.

Note from the Author

I'm honored to have had the chance to share with you what I feel most strongly about in this world. I know I've said it before, but I'll say it here again: Families are the building blocks of society. As women, wives, and mothers, along with husbands and fathers, we do important work when we nurture our families. Whatever else we do, and we as women do a lot else, we need to remember just how important the work of managing a family is. I have a lot of respect, admiration, and fondness for the many women I meet in the course of my work. In this book, I've shared a lot of their ideas and stories. I'd like to invite you to share your ideas and stories with me. In one of those five-minute time segments, with the note cards and stamps you now keep on hand, write me a note and let me know what's working for you. I'm only following my own advice in seeking help from the experts—all of you.

Also, if you'd like to schedule or inquire about a Family Manager Seminar in your area, please call (615) 376-5619. To receive the Family Manager newsletter, please send your name and address to:

Kathy Peel
c/o Family Manager
P.O. Box 50577
Nashville, TN 37205
FamilyManager@CompuServe.com

About the Author

Kathy Peel is the bestselling author of thirteen books, which have sold over 1.2 million copies. She is the founder and president of The Family Manager, a company committed to providing helpful ideas and resources to strengthen busy families and enhance the home.

She is the founder and editor-in-chief of *Family Manager* magazine and serves on the staff of *Family Circle* magazine. She speaks frequently at conferences and conventions and is a popular guest on television and radio programs. She has been featured in numerous newspapers and magazines and serves as the spokesperson for Day Runner.

Kathy Peel has been married for twenty-five years and is the mother of three boys, ages twenty-two, nineteen, and eleven.

To be a Family Manager, you need the know-how and the tools to get the job done right. The new Home Manager Organizer from Day Runner® helps manage family schedules and improve household communication — all in one neat package on your refrigerator. It comes in blue, green and white, and mounts easily on the fridge with slam-proof magnets.

The Home Manager Organizer features:
- A dated calendar with ample room for appointments and events
- A write and wipe board for family messages
- Post-it® Notes for jotting down phone numbers and shopping lists (not all models)
- A cork board or file pocket for holding coupons, invitations and important papers

The Home Manager Organizer can be found at warehouse clubs, discount department stores and office products superstores. For a Day Runner dealer near you, call 1-800-635-5544.